If you're a leader who's weary of bluster and preening and you long for an honest, faithful voice to name the ache in your soul, you've found a friend in Mandy Smith. These pages take us deep into our story, into our fear and hope, into the places where God waits for us with open arms.

WINN COLLIER, director of the Eugene Peterson Center for Christian Imagination and author of *Love Big, Be Well* and *A Burning in My Bones*

Like Mandy Smith's previous books, this is a searingly honest confession by a truly vulnerable pastor. Dr. Smith acknowledges her impulse to desire success, certainty, and comfort but shares how she has come to yearn for a different perspective—one that sees what God sees, glimpses what God is doing, and tries to follow the prompts of the Spirit. If you're like me, you'll be deeply disquieted by *Confessions of an Amateur Saint*. It's scary. Scary good.

MICHAEL FROST, Morling College, Sydney

What Mandy offers here ought to be self-evident among those who work in churches or in positions of spiritual influence, but sadly it is not. We have lost the art of true spiritual leadership, of what it means to be an elder in the church. We lean too heavily on secular skills and perspectives in our work of ministry and not enough on the sheer act of faith. Mandy challenges us to return to the vulnerable, messy, courageous work of real leadership after the pattern of Jesus. It is a call worth hearing and leaning into because the world starves for more truly spiritual leaders.

CAROLYN MOORE, pastor and church planter

Mandy Smith has done it again. She has honestly, creatively, and faithfully drawn us into things that matter most. Her searching self-examination as a pastor and as a woman leader during these turbulent days is itself richly reflective as she names and explores the familiar and the mysterious about the church and beyond. All this occurs as her undergirding sense of hope grounds her wisdom and faith. Mandy Smith is such a gift, and I consider myself her student. I commend you to do the same.

MARK LABBERTON, professor and president emeritus of Fuller Theological Seminary

This book is for those of us who love doi struggle with the tension of living in our relational style, Smith invites us to be rea difficulties of leadership, whether we're st

T0203549

to succeed, or other challenges. But she doesn't leave us there. She reminds us to return to our faith by confessing and choosing God rather than relying on ourselves. A wonderful, helpful book for strengthening and discipling Christian leaders.

MARYKATE MORSE, professor and author of *Lifelong Leadership* and *A Guidebook to Prayer*

We live in a world that teaches, "Blessed are the self-confident, for they will bring about the Kingdom of Heaven." But what if as we grow in ministry competencies, we become less self-reliant? Mandy shares her struggle to trust God in the daily grind of ministry and invites us on a journey to discover the countercultural truth that Jesus pronounced: "Blessed are the poor in spirit, for theirs is the Kingdom of Heaven."

JR WOODWARD, PhD, national director of the V3 Movement and author of *The Scandal of Leadership*

This beautiful book is a gift to us all! Mandy Smith writes with a tender vulnerability as a fellow believer who doesn't always fully believe but who chooses to keep trusting in God over and over through the practice of confession. She models this honest confession through personal stories, reflective exercises, and prayers that open us up to the transformative power of God in our lives and ministry. I believe this way of confession is the way of God-reliance and the way to abundant life!

JOYCE KOO DALRYMPLE, founder and director of Refuge for Strength; author

Thousands of pastors are discouraged and burned out. Many are looking for a way out. But what if there is a way *in*, a way to do ministry as a divine partnership marked by faith, confidence, and soul rest? In *Confessions of an Amateur Saint*, Mandy Smith shows us how. She reveals the practical benefit and joy of doing ministry through renewing our faith and refreshing our relational reliance on the presence and power of God.

BISHOP TODD HUNTER, author of *What Jesus Intended*

Mandy Smith is right; our world has shifted, and pastors are left in an "empty space, holding tools that no longer work, speaking words that have lost all meaning." If you're in this place and want out, follow her honest and creative lead as she models a way back to a faith that is authentic, empowered, and free.

JOHN VAN SLOTEN, community theologian and author of *God Speaks Science*

A courageous journey into the depths of the human soul. With profound vulnerability, Mandy Smith reveals the struggles and doubts that often accompany Christian leadership. Through her own confessions, she dismantles the barriers that separate us from God and invites us to join her in embracing our own vulnerability before the One who brings light in the darkness. If your soul feels burdened by the weight of trying to be more than an amateur saint, delve into this book and join the chorus of confession to discover the freedom that comes from embracing reliance on God.

LISA RODRIGUEZ-WATSON, national director of Missio Alliance

How can our sincere efforts as Christian leaders to be good at ministry make us very bad at ministry? Mandy Smith gently asks us to consider how we became so good at our jobs that we can do them without the enlivening work of God. *Confessions of an Amateur Saint* invites us to exchange professional competence for the practices of a robust, personal, and messy faith that reveals the work of God in the world. Even better, Mandy lives the life she describes and is an authentic guide.

TRISHA TAYLOR and JIM HERRINGTON, coauthors of *The Leader's Journey*

Mandy Smith is a necessary gift to us all because she generously invites us into her inner world and helps us feel seen and understood by making her own confessions. I find following an invisible God difficult, but Mandy has become a trusted guide for my own faith, and *Confessions of an Amateur Saint* is vintage Mandy Smith, one of the rare pastor-artists writing today.

STEVE CUSS, author and pastor

Mandy Smith is one of the wisest writers on church leadership today. Building on her previous books, *Confessions of an Amateur Saint* overflows with a keen sense of what it means to be human and to lead a church in these tumultuous times. Every pastor should read this book!

C. CHRISTOPHER SMITH, author of *How the Body of Christ Talks*

In this somewhat autobiographical book, our friend Mandy manages to communicate not just ideas that are helpful but something of her very precious self. Her *Confessions* are painfully honest, spiritually insightful, and pastorally authentic—the (in)credible witness of the quintessential amateur saint that is Mandy Smith.

DEBRA and ALAN HIRSCH, missional leaders, founders of Forge Mission Training Network and Movement Leaders Collective, and authors of various books

Good night. Mandy Smith has done it again. Few have the power to read my mail the way that Mandy does. This book invites the reader into a form of vulnerability and frailty that is almost uncomfortable. Through that vulnerability is the power of Christ. But we don't get to Christ by puffing ourselves up. We can only come broken. Mandy has shown us the way.

A.J. SWOBODA, PhD, professor of Bible and theology at Bushnell University and author of *The Gift of Thorns*

Almost every epistle in the New Testament is addressed to "the saints" and was penned as the early church was being established and formed. And yet the letters were clearly written to far-from-perfect people who were flawed in both theology and behavior, a reminder that to be a saint is to be a lifelong student in the way of Jesus: becoming the people God declares us to be.

In this book—which reads like a glimpse into a personal journal—Mandy Smith gently invites church leaders out of the perils and pressures of a professionalized ministry by reestablishing us as forever rookies in the life of faith. Through the honesty of confessing rather than covering up our incompetencies, Mandy points us toward the reality of God's power being perfected in human weakness.

With every turn of the page, with every confession of my own, I found myself being invited into the gift of identifying my own vulnerabilities, resulting in a deepening dependency on and intimacy with God—the goal of all saints.

ERIC E. PETERSON, pastor of Colbert Presbyterian Church

Years ago Mandy Smith wrote an exceptionally important book called *The Vulnerable Pastor* about ministers being real—honest about their fears and doubts and weakness. Here in *Confessions of an Amateur Saint* she shows us exactly what she means and how it is done, modeling a painful vulnerability that is rare, especially among professionally trained clergy. I came away stunned, amazed, a bit disturbed, and very, very grateful. I promise you have never read a book like this. Her creatively written meditations, laments, questions, and prayers reveal a deep longing for God and candor about the hard stuff of life and ministry. *Confessions* invites you to own up to your own struggles that, when named, will lead to healing and hope. Vital for pastors and truly useful for all.

BYRON BORGER, owner of Hearts & Minds, an independent bookstore in Dallastown, Pennsylvania

CONFESSIONS OF AN
AMATEUR SAINT

THE CHRISTIAN LEADER'S JOURNEY FROM
SELF-SUFFICIENCY TO RELIANCE ON GOD

A NavPress resource published in alliance
with Tyndale House Publishers

MANDY SMITH

NavPress.com

Confessions of an Amateur Saint: The Christian Leader's Journey from Self-Sufficiency to Reliance on God

Copyright © 2024 by Amanda Smith. All rights reserved.

A NavPress resource published in alliance with Tyndale House Publishers

NavPress and the NavPress logo are registered trademarks of NavPress, The Navigators, Colorado Springs, CO. *Tyndale* is a registered trademark of Tyndale House Ministries. Absence of ® in connection with marks of NavPress or other parties does not indicate an absence of registration of those marks.

The Team:
David Zimmerman, Publisher; Deborah Sáenz Gonzalez, Acquisitions Editor; Elizabeth Schroll, Copyeditor; Olivia Eldredge, Managing Editor; Dean H. Renninger, Designer; Sarah K. Johnson, Proofreading Coordinator

Cover and interior photograph of pianist and singer copyright © 1928 by Ernst Ludwig Kirchner (print in high resolution). Original from the National Gallery of Art. Digitally enhanced by Rawpixel (public domain). All rights reserved.

Interior artwork provided by the author and used with permission.

Author photo copyright © 2020 by Sarah Topp. All rights reserved.

Unless otherwise indicated, all Scripture quotations are taken from the *Holy Bible*, New Living Translation, copyright © 1996, 2004, 2015 by Tyndale House Foundation. Used by permission of Tyndale House Publishers, Carol Stream, Illinois 60188. All rights reserved. Scripture quotations marked NIV are taken from the Holy Bible, *New International Version,*® *NIV.*® Copyright © 1973, 1978, 1984, 2011 by Biblica, Inc.® Used by permission. All rights reserved worldwide. Scripture quotations marked NRSV are taken from the New Revised Standard Version Bible, copyright © 1989 National Council of the Churches of Christ in the United States of America. Used by permission. All rights reserved worldwide.

Published in association with Don Pape, curator at Pape Commons. papecommons.com

Some of the anecdotal illustrations in this book are true to life and are included with the permission of the persons involved. All other illustrations are composites of real situations, and any resemblance to people living or dead is purely coincidental.

For information about special discounts for bulk purchases, please contact Tyndale House Publishers at csresponse@tyndale.com, or call 1-855-277-9400.

ISBN 978-1-64158-837-9

Printed in the United States of America

30	29	28	27	26	25	24
7	6	5	4	3	2	1

For my friend Winn.
The way you follow helps me follow.
The way you lead helps me lead.

CONTENTS

FOREWORD

It's probably always been true at some level, but it's acute for us late-modern humans: We are prisoners of the moment. Perspective, particularly a historical one, is hard to come by. Our anxieties give us the assumption that our times are singularly troublesome. We come to believe that no one has dealt with the troubles we face. Particularly not the church.

I hear it often from pastors, bishops, and lay leaders. They say things like "The church has never faced such a challenge!" or "If we don't get our act together, the church is doomed" or "If we don't come up with new ways of being church there will be no church." But this just can't be true. It particularly can't be true theologically. Of course, the church is stewarded by fallible and sinful human beings, but the church exists because of God's act—alone! Therefore, like it or not (and I think at most times it's *not*), the church is God's responsibility. Not yours. Whether a pastor, bishop, or lay leader, we'd all do well to remember this. Nothing we do will save the church, for the church exists to witness to the fact that God alone is saving the world.

But how can we trust this? These may be nice if not terrifying thoughts. "But . . . b-b-but . . . b-b-but," we say to one another, "things are really bad. Never worse!" But that's not true either.

No one—never ever—would accuse me of being Mr. Brightside or Pollyanna Andy. Kierkegaard's biblical existentialism and Luther's theologia crucis run too freely in the veins of my imagination. I am not merely placating anxiety when I say that even with the propensity to think things through the negative (the via negativa), I know there have been worse times for the church. The late fourteenth and early fifteenth centuries come to mind. These were very bad times. France and England were in the middle of the Hundred Years' War; climate change from the Medieval Warm Period to the Little Ice Age was causing famine (there were years that summer never came); politics was heated, with dukes killing each other in the name of God; the church was divided between two popes (one in Rome and one in Avignon); and then, to really bring the crisis to a scream, one-third of Europe's population was wiped out by the bubonic plague. *Those* were some hard years! And yet the church survived. Our times of apathy and declining resources have their challenges, but the crisis is a bit less—a lot less—severe than in the fourteenth century.

But what we can learn from the crisis of the fourteenth century is not only to have some perspective but also that it's inside such perceived crises that calls for pastoral renewal arrive. Inside these times of crisis, when the pastoral task is most needed, we begin moving toward the renewal. The renewal often is bound to a reimagining of the pastoral task. The reimagining starts with a lonely prophet or two speaking against the tide.

In the late fourteenth century, that person was the child of peasants, who made it all the way to the University of Paris, and not just as a student, but eventually as chancellor. That man was the mystic Jean Gerson. As chancellor of the University of Paris, Gerson pushed the French king to end the schism of the two popes and sought to reform the university to educate pastors who could care for ordinary peoples' experiences of loss and fear. Gerson wanted the university not only to prepare priests for monasteries but more so to prepare pastors to wrestle with the presence and absence of God in people's lives. Gerson's efforts would be frustrated, eventually pushing him into exile. In exile he wrote his most important piece, *The Consolation of Theology.* In it Gerson claimed that the pastor's primary vocation is to walk with people through the pilgrimage of their lives, helping the whole of their lives be directed toward a living God. The pastor's job, Gerson assured, isn't just to operate the apparatus of the church's sacraments but to give people a glimpse of God's real action in the world, which comes near them in their sorrowing, bringing life out of death.

Mandy Smith is just the kind of pastor that Gerson imagined. She is a prophet—speaking against the current—for truly theological pastor renewal. In this book you're holding, Mandy offers us a call to renew pastoral identity and practice in a way that Gerson would've loved. Mandy is calling us back to a living God, who meets us not in our clerical assurances or doctrinal purity but right at the place where the God of Israel ministers, in our places of fear and trembling, in our doubts and faith. Gerson believed that if we leaned into our sorrows we'd find the presence of the God of life, ministering to us. Mandy wants something similar. She wants us to attend to our own yearning for a living God, to see whether, in our doubts and anxiety about the difficulty of the pastoral vocation, we might find the living God at work. And just maybe this living God will release us from our weariness to give us new life in the Spirit.

Our contemporary temptations, however, are much different from those of Gerson's day. We feel burdened with finding new ways to fix our problems. We need innovation, new strategies, new educational modules, new funding mechanisms, something new to fix our problems. Where Mandy's book is so important is in challenging this very assumption. She gives us no new programs, no new methods, no new identities as tech-savvy innovators. Instead, she reminds us of our *call*. Like Augustine, she calls us back to right our loves, directing those loves to God and God's people. Ultimately, she calls us back to loving and wrestling with God, believing that in pastoring people—in that same fear and doubt, hope and faith—God will truly and really move. *Confessions of an Amateur Saint* is an important book and one I believe will start a new genre we desperately need in Protestant pastoral reflections. This is a book by a practicing pastor discussing her wrestling with the living God. It's a gift to us all.

DR. ANDREW ROOT
author and professor at Luther Seminary

INTRODUCTION
A PROFESSIONAL PROBLEM (AND A NEW POSSIBILITY)

The structures of the modern world implicitly promise that we can operate as leaders, even as Christian leaders, without thought or need for God. Instead of our foundation being in Christ and His kingdom's way of influence, we rest on the cultural foundation set by the modern world of what it is to lead. We measure leadership with earthly definitions of success and power. A secular autopilot version of Christian leadership takes hold, where we lead like practical atheists, with God as an afterthought.

MARK SAYERS, *A NON-ANXIOUS PRESENCE*

I was dismayed at the growing disconnect between the spiritual and organizational lives of congregations. . . . It was rarely evident that I was working in a faith-based environment. . . . My clients were working in overdrive to reverse decline and improve organizational effectiveness. Few were engaging God as a partner in the striving.

SUSAN BEAUMONT, *HOW TO LEAD WHEN YOU DON'T KNOW WHERE YOU'RE GOING*

Something's wrong. Really wrong.

Christian leaders are dropping like flies. Those who aren't stepping away from Christian faith or leaving the profession are worn out, depressed, overwhelmed. We hear statistics about their health, their marriages, their addictions and vices, their abuses of power. We shake our fingers at them for letting us down. Of course they should be held accountable for their choices. At the same time, Christian leaders are canaries in a coal mine. Every time another one drops off their perch, we ask, "Why weren't they holding on more tightly?" How could we also be asking, "What's wrong with the coal mine?"

This is about the integrity of individuals. But it's bigger than that. There's something in our profession itself that is lacking in integrity—what it claims to be conflicts with what it actually is. The crisis of leaders burning out and having moral failings and losing faith and going on ego trips and abusing parishioners deserves attention. How can we also attend to the greater crisis? Little will change as long as we focus on the symptoms without also attending to the underlying sickness.

This inherent lack of integrity in Christian leadership has something to do with the fact that, like all professional people, we're supposed to be experts at something. But in our efforts to be good at preaching, making decisions, casting vision, we, too, often become incompetent in the very thing we're supposed to be good at—trusting that ultimately Someone Else is doing the work. And so, in a terrible irony, our efforts to be good at our job have often made us very bad at our actual job.

Professor Andrew Root knows how to name the crisis:

Ministry is too often seen as some function or professional action done by clergy; just as a clerk files papers or a programmer writes code, so a pastor ministers. It is the name of the core function of a profession. And as such, it is just a generic description of some *human* action. But . . . ministry is the very event that unveils *God's* action in the world. . . .

. . . In our secular age, divine action often seems

unbelievable. . . . [Ministers can become] more concerned with institutional structures (and the anxiety of their failing) than with an experience with God. The pastor either becomes the guardian and custodian of declining religion or needs to reinvent himself or herself as a religious entrepreneur, connecting busy, disinterested people with the programs and products of a church.[1]

Here, hidden in the crisis, is an opportunity. If it's the role of the minister to unveil God's action in the world, perhaps the best "skill" we can bring to this "profession" is to be really good at following God and at describing that following to others in a way that extends God's invitation. Perhaps the crisis itself will teach us our need for God more than ever so we will have what we actually need to do this work and what the world is actually longing to see from the church!

The Challenge of Leading from Faith

It seems patently obvious to say that Christian leaders should lead from faith. But I'm surprised to find how much it stretches me to (without apology) make decisions, lead meetings, cast vision, and preach sermons with regular reference to my own personal trust in God. It's remarkable to note how little of my development for Christian leadership trained me in the skills of leading from faith. Instead, I had many cautions to guard my congregation from my own subjective experiences of God. Of course, there are abusive ways to speak from faith as a leader, ways that manipulate others or that draw attention to ourselves. But have we overcorrected?

As we learn professional language and skills, there's an assumption that we also know how to lead from faith. Through decades of reading, studying, and attending leadership conferences, I've been trained in strategies, programs, and decision-making skills but never had training in how to bring my personal engagement with God into my work in a healthy, meaningful way. Twenty-five years into ministry, I'm coming to see just how much my personal faith is the thing that keeps me going in this impossible work. And how often honest expressions of faith are the place where God brings life to me and my ministry.

In recent years there's been much helpful analysis of "McDonaldization," the theory that modern society emulates this ubiquitous fast-food chain in highly valuing efficiency, predictability, calculability (quantifiable results), and (the illusion of) control.[2] In the critique of how these values have damaged the church, the conversation has largely been related to strategies and programs and less about how McDonaldization has affected the role and expectations of Christian leaders. If the church has become a factory, leaders have become cogs in the machinery—human beings whose flesh is pinched in the workings of the subhuman values of industrialization. We feel pressure to be predictable and tidy, to be self-contained and complete, to become bland, neutral, void of personality. Secular professionalism requires a self-sufficient competence that polishes us into a self-contained product, a finely tuned component precision-engineered to function in a machine.

When we bring that kind of professionalism into ministry, we find our work and church drained of the messiness, quirkiness, complexity, and beauty of what it means to be human. In their efforts to provide a consistent product, orange juice manufacturers freeze and distill fresh juice to make concentrate, boiling out the unique flavor that once told where each orange grew and how the weather was that year. It guarantees predictably mediocre orange juice. How can we hope for our people to enjoy the vitality of this faith if, in the name of consistency, we offer them a distilled version of our own experience of God? As pastor and theologian Eugene Peterson put it: "The secularized mind is terrorized by mysteries. Thus it makes lists, labels people, assigns roles, and solves problems. But a solved life is a reduced life."[3]

It's our professional calling to tell the story of a God who made it personal by personally stepping into our world, offered his Spirit to live in our very bodies. It's our profession to embody our personal faith in that story and invite others to take it personally, to retain the amateur's love for this, even as we gain professional skills. It will stretch us to figure out how to do that without abuse, but it's worth the risk.

What if our call is to strengthen others in their faith by inviting them to step with us into the risk of unknowing? What if the best way they'll see God at work is by having our company as we watch for him together?

Perhaps the best thing we can bring to a meeting is the skill of discerning when it's time to stop talking, stop spiraling, stop strategizing.

Perhaps the best skill we can bring to a crisis is knowing when it's time to reach beyond ourselves to pray.

Maybe the best communication skill we can have is the capacity to share living stories of actual dependence on God.

Perhaps the best strategy we can offer is the determination to keep listening to God and saying yes, every step of the way, knowing only too well how unprofessional that might sound.

We may find that the most professional skill we can bring is knowing how to stop being so good at our job that no one needs God. The ways we're learning to follow God personally might also be essential to the ways we lead others, inviting them to trust with us.

As much as we can shape structures and programs, we cannot control the people—their choices to attend, to serve, to give, to grow. But we do know how someone becomes a disciple because we've been doing that all our Christian lives. We know it's not our own work but work being done in us. We don't have to understand it. We're not expected to always feel it or even fully believe it. But we can control our will. We can choose once more to say yes, day after day. If this is what it means to follow God personally, why not also trust we can follow God in this way professionally?

For many of us the call to ministry began with a deep, personal longing for or encounter with God. We were amateurs doing this for the love of it.[4]

For me, the call to ministry felt at first like an invitation to hide, full-time, in the comfort of God's presence. But ministry is so far from comfortable that I've learned to wryly forewarn my doctor of ministry students: "Don't let my appearance of comfort fool you. I'm not comfortable. It's just that I'm getting used to the discomfort." (*Discomfort* is not nearly a strong enough word for what can feel like relational, social, and existential death. Day after day.)

Instead of leading to the comfort I expected, my ministry has been twenty-five years of pioneering, whether because I'm from a different country or a different denomination or because I'm the first woman to lead in a particular place. How did this desire for comfort lead me to the role of reluctant change agent? And at a time of great upheaval in our culture and church, I'm not alone—we're all pioneers now, whether we like it or not.

Pioneering looks very little like maintaining the status quo and requires a watchful adventurousness that doesn't look much like "profession." We may be discipled in these risky, adaptive skills in our personal faith—have we been given permission to bring them into our profession? Now more than ever, our profession looks very little like certainty (unless you count certainty in God).

This reality seems cruel according to the world's way of having a career—we've been given an impossible task to lead something without really knowing what on earth it is or will become. But this work promises to teach us the very skills required for the work.

If we approach ministry through the lens of discipleship, the challenges of this work teach us this essential skill of following

God. (And we have much to learn from those who follow him even though it's not their job!) Viewed through the lens of secular professionalism, every question, every problem is a sign we need more consultants, conferences, and strategies. But in professional pioneering we recognize questions and problems and upheaval as a chance to rely more on God. So the work of leading others in their discipleship is a fundamental lesson we learn ourselves even in the act of leading them. Leading from faith no longer pulls us in warring directions but becomes a way of deep integrity.

Our call is to be strong in our ability to turn to God, not to be strong in ourselves.

To stretch out our roots and branches to take in life from God, not to be self-sufficient.

To share how it's messy, how it stretches our perseverance.

To be able to say, "I don't know what God will do, but I know what he can do."

Our profession is confessional—confessing to God the ways we're tempted toward self-reliance and confessing once more our reliance on him. In a secular, post-everything age, what the world most needs to see from the church is our own reliance on the power of a transcendent God. Do we, as products of this age, even know how to rely like that?

This leading from faith does not mean always feeling God's presence, always knowing God's direction, but rather making a faithful choice day after day. We can't control our understanding or emotions, but we can control our will, choosing God yet one more time. And another time after that. And we can choose to share what we find there. May we become proficient at the right things. And when we do, a world disillusioned by the failures of secularism will sit up to see one small, human face lit up with belief in the living God. A cynical, postmodern world devoid of grand narratives will be intrigued by one person's subjective, messy, wonderful story of a God at work in their days.

CHAPTER ONE

CONFESSING UNBELIEF, CONFESSING BELIEF

We act like pagans in a crisis.

OSWALD CHAMBERS, *MY UTMOST FOR HIS HIGHEST*

To whom am I telling this story? It isn't of course to you, my God, but in your presence I'm telling it to my race, the human race. . . . And what's the story's purpose? Obviously, it's so that I and whoever reads this can contemplate from what depths we must cry out to you. But what's closer to your ears, if the heart humbles itself in confession and the life is lived in faith?

AUGUSTINE, *CONFESSIONS*

I confess.

I confess I don't believe in God.

Well, if belief is a cognitive assent, I guess I do believe. I assent to the idea of God. I'm willing to acknowledge God exists.

But I don't believe God is present.

And I don't believe God is powerful.

And I don't believe God is benevolent.

I don't believe God is acting right here and now in this place, in this body, in this Body.

If behavior attests to belief, I don't believe.

Oh, I'm a Christian. A pretty Christian Christian. You could say I have been all my life: born to Christian parents and Christian grandparents. We prayed before meals, talked about God, went to church every week. When I was small enough to sit in my mother's lap in church and lay my head on her chest, I heard the sound of the singing resonating in her body and wondered if all the church was in her. My dad's faith brought tears to his eyes, making me wonder, *What is so powerful that it humbles the most powerful person I know?* This was not just learning ideas but the embodied experience of Jesus alive in my life and my home and community, modeling for me a way of life that turned the other cheek and welcomed strangers. It was so much a part of my development that my wedding was also an ordination, blessing us not only to a life submitted to one another but also to God. And for the past twenty-five years I've devoted myself to that life. I pray, I read the Bible, I talk a lot about God.

But I'm also secular. As much as I was steeped in bodily experiences that grew from the way of Jesus, I've been shaped by secular liturgies.[1] I've been molded by a culture that was influenced enough by Christianity to seem Christian enough, been educated by institutions with good, inclusive values, led by politicians who valued freedom and democracy, trained by media that seemed a harmless distraction. These have fed me as much as the bread and wine. I've been as immersed in them as in the waters of baptism. As positive as they may in some ways be, they're not founded on a fundamental belief in a transcendent being. And so, alongside my father's tears and my mother's songs and my Bible college classes, I've been shaped to be self-reliant. And to be ashamed when I'm not. My eyes have taken in countless ads whose main message is that something's wrong with me and I need to fix it. I've sat in countless classrooms that have taught me I can find an answer to every question if I study long enough. I've been influenced by leaders who think it's their job to be my savior (and intuited that when I lead, I'll need to become a savior too). As much as we bundle the kids off to Sunday school and listen to Christian radio and tattoo ourselves with Bible verses, we're secular saints.

If belief means writing sermons by looking up from my laptop and toward the Writer of every sermon, on Wednesday mornings I often don't believe.

If belief means remembering that Someone Else birthed and nurtures this congregation, too many Sundays I don't believe.

If belief means leading every meeting knowing every breath around the table is breathed in his Spirit, I regularly don't believe.

If belief means obeying regardless of how it will affect others' opinions of me, too often I don't believe.

If belief means remembering that my daily desperation is an invitation to reach outside myself, most days I don't believe.

If belief means choosing not to do the quick, violent thing with my pain, right now I don't believe.

For every question I don't bring to him, every meeting I don't invite him into, every crisis I try to resolve in my own strength, I don't believe.

Me, a pastor, who's supposed to help people believe!

Oh, I have my moments. Moments when I remember the things I claim and choose them once again. But for someone who has not only been living this Christian life for a long time but also been guiding others in it, it's amazing how often I'm an atheist. Of course, I would never say, "I am called to be this church's savior." But with the next crisis, my savior habits surface again:

Problem? Be powerful!

Question? Be present!

Crisis? Be active!

While I say, "I believe God is powerful and present and active," my behavior too often proclaims this theology:

I am powerful, *I* am present, and *I* am active.

And when I finally remember to reach outside myself to get resources—to ask questions, to find books and best practices—it's still too often an anxious grasping for tools that allow me to clamber back to self-sufficiency. My goals have been shaped by my following of Jesus. But my methods are too often shaped by my discipleship in the secular way of things. I'd never say it, but my life proclaims it loud and clear: I want to be a closed system. I'd like to be self-contained. Of course, I also want to flourish, to bear fruit. But it seems I must make a choice.

In Jeremiah 17 God offers a pretty stark choice to his people:

> Thus says the LORD:
> Cursed are those who trust in mere mortals
>   and make mere flesh their strength,
>   whose hearts turn away from the LORD.
> They shall be like a shrub in the desert,
>   and shall not see when relief comes.
> They shall live in the parched places of the wilderness,
>   in an uninhabited salt land.
>
> Blessed are those who trust in the LORD,
>   whose trust is the LORD.
> They shall be like a tree planted by water,
>   sending out its roots by the stream.
> It shall not fear when heat comes,
>   and its leaves shall stay green;
> in the year of drought it is not anxious,
>   and it does not cease to bear fruit.
>
> JEREMIAH 17:5-8, NRSV

This is not tit for tat. God's not saying, "If you reject me, I'll punish you." And it's also not prosperity gospel. He's not saying, "If you trust me, you'll never have problems (so if you have problems, you just don't have enough faith)." This is describing the natural outcome of our choices: Since God is the source of life, it's only natural that if we cut ourselves off from him, we'll begin to dry up.

Visualizing this image of two trees—one withered, one verdant—I know which kind of life I'd rather have. Of course

1. Contemplate this self-sufficient tree. It's a closed system, the opposite of the flourishing, reliant tree described in Jeremiah 17. How does it strike you? How long might this tree stay alive? Will it ever bear fruit? Will it ever birth new trees?

2. How are you like this tree? How do you rely on your own resources?

3. Where is God inviting you to stretch out to him for all you need? How does that feel?

I want to be unafraid in drought. I want leaves that are always green. I want to be ever fruitful. And so I set about doing whatever it takes to be sure I'm always flourishing, always fruitful. And without realizing it, I'm working hard to become the fruitful tree and inadvertently becoming the withered. The harder I work to be green, the more I "trust in mere mortals" and "make mere flesh [my] strength." So I shouldn't be surprised when I begin withering like the shrub in the desert. The *way* we go about finding life is what makes the difference. The choice is not whether we want to be dried up or flourishing—of course we'd all choose flourishing. The choice is where we place our trust, what is the source of our life.

It's a natural response—in anxiety, we shrink in. In desperation, it's a fundamental human self-preservation instinct to conserve energy, to tuck ourselves in tight. But this streamside tree keeps sending out roots, stretching, seeking, siphoning. And because of that stretching of roots deep, deep in the earth, it's able to also send out branches into the sky, drawing in rain and sun, burgeoning with leaves and life. The skyward yearning of its branches mirrors the subterranean yearning of its roots.

We say we believe in God. What does it mean to live as if he's literally, *actually* our source of life? How would we live if we really believed he's the answer to every question, the resolution of every crisis, the preacher of every sermon, the leader of every community? That kind of belief teaches us to watch for that old habit that sets our roots curling inward again and to choose to stretch out those roots once more. Oh, we'll need every capacity and gift we can muster. Each tree has the inherent capacity to grow, to bear fruit, to multiply. But none of these capacities are engaged without external nourishment. God does not ask us to be passive or to set aside our capacities. The question is whether God's capacity or our own is the source of our hope. When everything we've been taught by our culture, the media, our education (sometimes even our ministry training), tells us to depend on ourselves, this outward reaching feels like death.

But it looks like life.

And how it looks will be important. Because that tree by the stream does not just flourish for its own sake. Its flourishing is a witness. It's an impossible tree, a tree that makes no sense. In a dry and weary land this tree not only survives but thrives, bearing fruit and green leaves all year round, defying seasons. Encountering this tree, with all its vibrant life and color, is a burning-bush kind of moment, drawing us closer to investigate. How does this tree do it? What's going on here that's not true for the withered tree? This flourishing tree, verdant in drought, points to something outside itself. And because it doggedly remains reliant on that stream, it can be a resource, a place of shelter and nourishment, an oasis. It's alive for its own sake and for the sake of others.

As Christian leaders, we know it's our job to be a resource for others. So we take this work very seriously. The seriousness of it all has led me to seminary, to countless conferences and workshops. Too few of my mentors have let me see behind the scenes of their own wrestling and prayer and hope and perseverance. Too few leadership books describe the daily confessions, the weekly conversions. Since it's often our faith that draws us into this vocation, our training often assumes faith. My training has encouraged me toward helpful self-care practices that nurture my relationship with God. And I've had training in how to teach others about their own faith. But in all that training, reading, and resourcing, I haven't heard much about the tricky skill, the vital necessity of engaging my own faith in the daily work of leading a congregation. In fact, I've been warned many times not to "make it about me," to somehow serve other people's faith by rarely mentioning my own. I'm a chef who's been warned to restrain my delight in food. I'm just here to cook for others.

But this work stretches my faith beyond my comfort level on a daily basis, inviting me to proclaim things I can't see, to press toward goals we may never achieve, to claim hope when the world (and church) are crumbling, to speak challenge when I just want harmony. It stretches my fundamental sense of self-worth and identity, my desire to be known and liked, my need to be comfortable, my longing to know the future, my hunger to be part of something successful. It breaks and remakes me every day. And in it I get the feeling I'm slowly becoming more like Jesus.

What a possibility—that this work of helping others walk with Jesus might, if we pay attention, equip us in our own walk with Jesus! Those things that seem to overcome and disqualify us can, when approached with Jesus' willingness to be broken, make us new. The thing that threatens to undo us holds within it the very thing that might just remake us. The desperation of this impossible task of leading others into faith might just stretch our own faith so much that we'll have something to say. And it will light up our faces to say it. Not because it's easy but because there's Good News on the other side of despair. There's life hidden in what we feared might kill us.

We've found ourselves in a profession where we regularly feel unprofessional, stumbled into a career where we can't direct our own destiny. How can we grow in our capacity for the discomfort of this work? How can we get used to the fact that the best way to be good at this job is to know our need for something beyond ourselves? How can we rediscover faith in God (imperfect though our faith may be) as the foundational "skill" for this work? And how can we develop emerging leaders and resource existing leaders as if Jesus is still the actual head of his church and our best "best practice" is knowing how to listen to and partner with him?

My days are driven by the ache of not believing any of this as fully as I'd like. It drives me away from God and, in my better moments, also has the potential to drive me toward him. It's a constant struggle between my secular habits of independent competence and my Christian habits of dependence.

In the chapters that follow, I share these struggles, written on ordinary days. (*Written.* Such a tame word for what has felt more like throwing up. Or fighting for my life.) I share them not because I think my faith is remarkable. In fact, it's because it's so ordinary that I feel called to share. I share to invite others to name with me, and make public, this daily repentance, this regular rhythm of death and resurrection, to remember together this is what our call actually is, as leaders and as followers.

We may have signed up for a nice, stable, predictable job: The church has been around for centuries, the Bible is always the same, and God never changes. We may have expected to maintain an institution, to recite familiar passages, to cruise. And then the rug got pulled out from underneath us, and suddenly nothing that's "always worked" is working anymore. The words that have always been spoken suddenly sound like gibberish (or violence). The rooms that were once filled now echo; the practices we once knew are forgotten. And our profession is left in the empty space, holding tools that no longer work, speaking words that have lost all meaning. And this once-comfortable, predictable space now feels like an undiscovered planet, and we're gasping, hoping our lungs can learn to breathe new air. We're figuring out how to proclaim hope in a foreign tongue that's being formed as we speak it.

I'm a settler at heart. I found my husband and my calling before the age of twenty and thought I was set. Put me somewhere for a long time, let me set down roots, and I'll grow something. But look at my life and you'd never believe I have a settler's heart. Instead, I find myself a reluctant pioneer. Four international moves (three before the age of twenty-six) have stretched my settler's heart. The uprooting, the adapting, the making a home in a foreign place have given me no choice but to learn a pioneer kind of faith. Finding myself the first female lead pastor in a fellowship of six thousand congregations taught me pioneer perseverance.

Ministry to young adults in post-Christian contexts has taught me pioneer adaptivity. And doing the work of church planting and regeneration has required me to discover a pioneer's capacity for humility and failure. None of these were lessons I was asking for. All of them are lessons I'm still learning.

There are many kinds of pioneering. You may be a pioneer because you're new to your role, the first person your age or gender or race or from your background to lead here. The context may be (or seem) stable, but you're new or different (so you may feel the pioneering more than those around you). It may be that you're planting something new or reenvisioning something old. You may be casting a vision for something you have never even seen. You may be called to shape new definitions for what this faith, this church, this mission could be. And, likely, you'll feel the greater work that is going on in the global church, where the old best practices no longer work and the solid things we once relied on are no longer available or meaningful.

So regardless of the specifics of your place and your call, there are many dynamics that all pioneers must navigate. Here are a few of the many that you may be facing:

- Working within old denominational, theological, relational, or political systems that we must maintain even as we reimagine and reshape them. This can feel like the work of palliative care and midwifery at the same time!

- Shaping new language and new metaphors to pave new paths forward.

- Functioning in many roles, some of which you may not be gifted or experienced in, which means feeling constantly stretched, inadequate, and underprepared.

- Having to defend your decisions because they're unfamiliar to the people in this place (and maybe even having to teach people how to follow you).

- Taking risks to experiment with new ideas that have never been tried (at least not here or by you) and dealing with your own anxiety while reassuring others who are risk averse. Having many opportunities to fail, often publicly, while reassuring those around you (and yourself) that failure is not the worst thing that can happen.

- Feeling alone—and sometimes actually being alone—in the work, either because there are no others (yet) to help or because those who are there don't get the vision or don't (yet) have the capacity to participate. Feeling in desperate need of advocates and allies and assistants.

- Carrying a heavy load while also finding and developing others to help bear the load (which makes double work for you until others are ready to step up).

- Living in a place of incompleteness, rarely seeing outcomes or being fully assured of what the outcomes will be, daily investing in something that may or may not become what you expect (and inviting others into that thing that doesn't yet exist so that it can exist).

- Dealing with high levels of anxiety, which affects sleep, relationships, and health. (All this in the middle of an ordinary life that, like every life, has its own ups and downs, family conflicts, and health concerns.)

- Discerning your own false-self issues—your fears about performance, perfection, and/or pleasing everyone, which may trigger traumas and unhealthy appetites.

- Engaging with a high degree of spiritual warfare.

In all this upheaval we have a choice. We can continue our secular habits with their knee-jerk response of desperate scrambling for that elusive self-sufficiency. Or we can remember this faith we claim that calls us to reach beyond our own small selves one more time. It may require us to remember the ancient practice of confession—confessing our practical atheism and confessing once more our choice to trust in the power of God. We may find that this habit that feels like weakness will actually bring the very life we've been working so hard to attain.

If belief is an act of will, a choice to live as if God is good and active and present and powerful, then I choose to believe. I can't always force feelings of belief. I can't always alleviate my doubts. But I can choose to act. I can use my will to live the way I would live if belief were simple. I can trust that the feelings will come (and go again), the doubts will pass (and return), as I just try each day to make a few more choices toward actual reliance on God than I did the day before.

So I confess.

I confess I believe in God.

I confess belief in a God who is present and powerful and benevolent and at work here and now.

I confess belief that this God has not forsaken his church but has a hope and a future for her.

I confess I believe God's Spirit still transforms human hearts and communities.

I confess I believe God still speaks powerfully through Scripture.

I confess I believe God still works through ordinary, broken people.

I confess I believe that even in desert places, God is still making all things new.

Too often we have just two kinds of leadership models: the perfect ones who never seem to feel inadequate, never make mistakes, and the leaders who make abusive choices that take down whole ministries. I don't see myself in either. I need to watch ordinary leaders who feel the fear and choose God once more. I need to see behind the scenes of their dealings with their own self-sufficiency. I want to hear their very real temptations to be their own little god. I want to witness the moment they choose to need something beyond their own small selves.

In the middle of Paul's reasonable explanation of law and sin in Romans 7, he could have kept it abstract. Instead he chooses to say "I," and suddenly we're watching closely the personal dynamics of a human will. We want Paul to make the right choice, but we also don't want it to seem too easy—or else what good is his story for our struggles? The very words themselves tumble over one another: "What I want to do I do not do. . . . I do not do the good I want to do, but the evil I do not want to do—this I keep on doing" (verses 15, 19, NIV).

I do. I do. I do.

I. I. I.

Do. Do. Do.

At last, the impossibility of "I do" has brought Paul to a new subject—from "I" to "who"—and a new action—from "do" to "rescue" (verse 24, NIV). The dryness of desperation has itself become an opportunity to reach beyond this closed system. When the despair of our insufficiency feels most like death, there's relief in simply remembering that there is life outside of us:

"Thanks be to God, who delivers me . . . !" (verse 25, NIV).

I do. But God delivers.

Every morning dawns with new temptations to dominate the day. So every morning I walk and wrestle. By the end of every walk, I drop my keys by the door and head straight for the keyboard to bash out the confessions that can finally be expressed, a kind of convulsive purging of the daily desire to need nothing but my own self. And a choice once more to depend. It leaves me wrung out but free. I know that any flourishing in my life and ministry grows from those daily moments of repentance. So because I've found such companionship in Paul's confessions and such fruitfulness from following his example, I share these stories of thrashing and choosing and turning. The chapters that follow are collections of my morning confessions. In each confession you'll find both a confession of my temptation toward suffocating self-reliance and a confession of my choice to believe once more (sometimes little more than a choice to *want* to believe and a promise to live as if I do). And each chapter begins with an essay that explores how biblical characters wrestled with these temptations so we remember we're not alone.

"A life of faith" can sound like one solid lump of believing. But faith is not always fully believing. And "a life of faith" can sound like a choice we made once, a long time ago. But this life of faith is made up of minuscule choices to set aside our own small interpretations, to imagine light in darkness, to say yes when we'd rather say no (or no when we'd rather say yes), to choose to please an invisible God over the very visible faces surrounding us. This life asks us to risk when we want security, to give when we want to hoard, to believe Scripture over how the world seems to us. The stories I need to hear (and so choose to tell) are the stories of those small, significant moments to choose again.

Many of the stories are amalgams of various experiences in four different congregations in two different countries over twenty-five years. I've changed details to describe the kinds of situations a leader experiences. In places where the story is more specific to a particular person, I've asked their permission to share it. I often tell the specifics of the situation only so far because for me the circumstances are not the point. The real story is happening on the level of will—am I choosing to turn toward or away from God in this moment? Is my desperation a door to disbelief or one more opportunity for reliance? After all, as much as we talk about belief versus doubt, in Scripture, the contrast is often belief versus obedience. Belief is not held only in our heads but also in our hands and feet. As theologian Brenda Colijn explains: "Truth is not just something to be believed but something to be practiced. Believers must 'do the truth.'"[2]

Please don't read the confessions as a complete description of ministry. I'm not writing a general primer on the experience of Christian leadership. There are many times in ministry when it's easy to believe in God. I write confessions for all the other times. And in this pioneering season there are many of them. How we respond to those moments will shape the culture of our communities and decide the future of our movement. So it's vital that we're vigilant to detox from our secular habits, to remember our reliance on a power beyond our own. And at the same time, what a grace that although we get it wrong day after day, God is working—whether we remember him or not.

The confessions can be read through from beginning to end in the usual way of reading a book. I hope that together they describe one leader's life of wrestling every day for God-reliance. At the same time, I've given each confession a title based on the experience that tempted me to turn from God so that you can return to read them separately when you have similar circumstances.

Maybe one day we'll be less surprised that we can't be all we need.

Until then let's keep confessing.

Reflect

1. What was it that initially led you to Christian leadership? Was there an experience of God, a longing for something for his church? A hunger or a hope? Is that still in you? What shape does it take today? How can that primitive prompt (from before this was your profession) still be expressed in your work?

2. What are your concerns about leading from your own faith? What part of those concerns are healthy hesitations that keep you from crossing boundaries? What part of those concerns are an overreaction to abuses? For example: What might it look like to press into authority without domination? Or to share your own lessons in following God without making it about yourself? Or to invite the intimacy required in sharing behind the scenes of our faith without creating an unhealthy intimacy? And how can we discern healthy ways to protect ourselves from abuse as well, to avoid casting "pearls before swine" (Matthew 7:6, NRSV)?

3. What leadership models are you following? What models are you reacting to?

4. How are you seeing God shape you as a disciple in the crucible of Christian leadership? How does (or can) that experience, messy and painful though it may be, help you follow and lead?

5. In Philippians 4:9, Paul writes, "Whatever you have learned or received or heard from me, or seen in me—put it into practice" (NIV). And in 1 Corinthians 11:1: "Follow my example, as I follow the example of Christ" (NIV). Is this self-centeredness and pride? What is it that Paul's asking the believers in Philippi or Corinth to learn from him? How does it look to lead like this in your context?

6. What is the difference between a secular way of being good at a job and a Christian way?

CHAPTER TWO

I WANT TO BE IN CONTROL

God, of your goodness, give me yourself, for you are enough for me.
JULIAN OF NORWICH, *REVELATIONS OF DIVINE LOVE*

God makes promises. And then he waits. Sometimes for a really long time. Long enough for us to wonder if we imagined the promises. Long enough for us to wonder if he's forgotten them. Maybe we misheard? Maybe we misunderstood?

It could be said that the biggest promise God ever made to a person was his promise to Abram. So big it took the whole universe to describe it. So big it promised to burst beyond Abram's single life across time and space. God sings this promise to make one man into a whole nation, to bless all the peoples of the earth. And Abram believes it. But belief can wear thin.

I wonder how often Abram recounted the promise to his wife, Sarai. I wonder how many months she waited for the signs of change in her body before she became bitter with disappointment. Perhaps over time, she asked, "Tell me again exactly how he said it. How can you be the father of a nation without first being the father of a son? How can you be the father of a son unless I am the mother of a son?" Months turned to years, and the promise turned to dust in their mouths.

Who can say if Abram and Sarai even knew what it meant to be the seed of a nation? Who knows if they could even fathom the cosmic blessing they'd received? Like all people of their time, they just wanted to feel God's ordinary blessing of a child—someone to love, someone to care for you in your old age, someone to carry on your legacy. Is it so bad to want such things? After all, family is God's invention, and the desire to procreate is a God-given, human instinct. After ten years, the sweeping promises given under an open sky have shrunk. Ten years of waiting and disappointment, waiting and disappointment have become a maddening cycle. And now, in despair, Abram and Sarai see only one option: to take matters into their own hands.

I've been in that place. There's been a promise given, but can't God see all the ways it's impossible? I've waited a long time, but nothing's happened. I don't want to question God's power. I don't want to give up hope on the promise. But this is getting ridiculous. It would be easier to forget he ever said anything. It would be easier to stop anticipating—*is today the day? No? Maybe today?*

I see Sarai's logic: On the one hand, God has promised Abram he will be a father. On the other hand, as she puts it in Genesis 16:2, "The Lord has kept me from having children" (NIV). If these two truths exist, it's time to act, time to find a plan B. This cosmic plan for all the generations seems to have shriveled in one woman's body. So Sarai proposes a way to resolve the pain and tension (and in so doing creates new pain and tension). Her years of worrying and weeping in her tent have made the problem very local. This cosmic hope has become a personal failure of her body, her family. So she looks close at hand for the solution—her own maidservant and her own initiative: "Perhaps I can build a family through her" (Genesis 16:2, NIV).

I've been in that same place. I guess when God made the promise he forgot I'd have limited opportunities and limited resources. He didn't see how this person would block the path or that system would make the promise impossible. When God promised all nations would be blessed, he mustn't have known about the stupid decisions humans would make. When he said all things will be made new, he must have not factored in all the brokenness of the world. When he said the gates of hades would not prevail against his church, he obviously didn't foresee what's going on today. When he promised he's restoring all things, surely he didn't actually mean *all*.

When God doesn't get on with acting in the way he promised, the choice seems to be between giving up on the promise entirely and forcing the promise in our own strength. The harder choice is to trust he's working, in ways we cannot see, to ask each day, *What is my part in the promise and what is not?*

ALWAYS IN PROCESS

I have twelve documents open in various stages of completeness. I rarely turn off my computer for fear that one of these tabs or documents will not open again when the computer flickers back to life and it will drop off my screen—literally and metaphorically—forever. Even as I reach one milestone—the church is growing—now there are more milestones hidden behind that one: find and train someone to lead a children's ministry; create a new Bible study to meet new needs. If feeling confident in my success, feeling real as a person and a pastor, means pointing to outcomes, I'm just out of luck.

I feel like I'm tripping and catching myself, tripping and catching myself over and over. To the point that this is now my actual gait, not an upright, slow, and steady series of paces entirely in my control but this irregular dance set to no recognizable beat, never falling (well, actually, sometimes . . .) but never actually doing what would normally be called walking. A lunging forward to catch myself with every trip. Every stumble bringing the rise in my stomach and in my heart rate and every catch bringing the calming of relief for just a moment before the next stumble and my heart and stomach flutter once more.

But somehow we're moving forward. In this awkward tripping and catching, tripping and catching, we're getting somewhere. It's not my preferred way of getting somewhere, but is it possible I'm learning a kind of grace in it, even an embrace of the ridiculousness of it all? Maybe there are new muscles being toned in me, tiny tendons that normally go unused? Maybe my task is not to wish for a steady gait while doing whatever this strange other thing is. Maybe the invitation is for me to set aside my resistance, my desire to look competent and comfortable and in control.

Could it be that as I learn the flow of this unpredictable always tripping/always catching myself it becomes a spectacle that makes no sense? If I smile and wave as I move in this odd way, might it be a moment of wonder when others might say, "Well, you don't see that every day! It makes no sense: This person who is certainly going to fall flat on her face, who doesn't seem to know where she's going, is somehow getting somewhere!"?

Father,

I confess that I would much prefer a structured space where goals and outcomes are clear, where my tasks are set out for me and I'm able to measure results.

Would I trust you less in that kind of work?

Would I still ask for your help?

Would I lose the point of what I'm doing as it became an end in itself?

I hope that something significant would be different, since this way costs me dearly every day.

Will the discomfort be worth it?

May all the plans still in process, all the documents and sermons and emails and decisions yet incomplete, keep me on my toes for the tripping and catching.

May they keep my eyes on you if for no other reason than because I have nothing else.

Amen.

"If . . . you sometimes fall, do not lose heart, or cease striving to make progress, for even out of your fall God will bring good."[1]

SAINT TERESA OF ÁVILA

Write Your Own Confession

1.   How do you feel always in process?

2.   How does it tempt you toward self-sufficiency? Confess it in all its ugliness.

3.   How do you choose to trust God instead, even if it means you won't get what you'd rather have?

IN KNOTS

I have knots in my stomach. Four, to be precise. Three on the left side of my body, one on the right.

I don't feel them all the time, but I notice them when I lie in bed. It feels like the butterflies in my stomach have turned to concrete, no longer delicate wings that could almost be mistaken for excitement. Heavy, stone lumps. Literal, actual hard spots of twisted fascia or muscle or something. I've heard various explanations from physical therapists who have alleviated them temporarily, but the knots always return.

I'm familiar with the knots we can get in our shoulders from postural habits. I have what I call a "writer's knot" between my spine and right shoulder blade. No amount of pressing on it can keep up with my habit of hovering that hand over the mouse pad. But that knot doesn't concern me.

Unlike the stomach knots. I've had all the scans. They aren't going to kill me. But I have to wonder: What posture is causing these to build? I sense it's more a posture of will and heart and mind than anything that could be fixed with a standing desk or a Pilates class.

I can only guess at what draws sinews into hardness. I've noticed the knots turn up most when I'm feeling called to places I'd rather not go. The first year they appeared was a year I felt a new voice rising in me, stretching me to set aside my lifelong habits of deference and silence. That year I also felt invited to publicly pray for healing for someone I could hardly imagine healed.

That summer our family went hiking at the same place we'd hiked every summer, ending with sandwiches on a rather precarious precipice. Every previous year I'd sat close to the edge and happily munched my sandwich. This year the physical pain was too great, building deep in my stomach with every step closer to the summit. As I sat that day, puzzled at the change in myself, I reflected on what had changed. That year I'd often said I felt God calling me to edge out on a limb. As soon as I became accustomed to the swaying of the limb, he'd called me out farther still.

I'd rather stay on the ground, marveling from safety at the loveliness of the tree above. It wasn't my idea to shimmy up and out onto a branch, then farther out and farther still and farther. It isn't my preference that this branch also happens to be stretching out over a precipice. It isn't ideal that the wind is beginning to pick up and the swaying is no longer fun. I want to inch back to safety, but I feel called to stay here, proclaiming things I hardly understand, moving toward things that get me unliked, hoping in things that could disappoint me.

> God,
>
> Did you have knots in your stomach when you walked around in human form? Did you feel the pressing in of all that threatens human existence, all that rankles our comfort?
>
> Did you feel that temptation to preserve yourself? Did you want to keep yourself alive and well-liked and in charge of your future? Did you want to avoid making big claims and sticking your neck out? Were you tempted to stay safe, to defer and conform?
>
> Whatever you had that allowed you to keep being obedient, to keep dying to your preference for comfort and convenience, can you share some of it with me?
>
> All things are possible for you. Take these knots from me. But not my will, but yours.
>
> And if they're a kind of thorn in the flesh, let me know how your grace is sufficient.
>
> Amen.

"What if you were falling forever, what would you do? Well, for the first few hundred years or so you'd go, 'Aaaaagghhh!' But you can get bored with being terrified. You can exhaust the limits of terror and fear and anxiety. Then what would you do? Falling, falling, falling. You might turn somersaults. You might sing. Now what if there were such a thing as a groundless jump? Then fear would be groundless, literally. And what if life is a groundless jump?"[2]

JAMES FINLEY

Write Your Own Confession

1. Are there ways your body carries the pain and anxieties inherent in this work?

2. What kind of confession do you need to frame to trust God in that?

3. What kind of confession might allow you to invite God into that place in your body?

BEYOND A REASONABLE RISK

It's time to do something here. "Fish or cut bait," whatever that means. Everything I do feels like making do with not enough, but this is beyond that. I know it's my job to jump in with both feet, cast the vision with hope and enthusiasm. But I genuinely don't know if this is even a good risk. There are times when we have to override reason and times when we have to listen to it. All my reason says, *We don't have what we need to even imagine a new thing.* Reasonably, we don't have enough people, enough resources, enough finances, enough time, enough "energy" or "momentum" or "buy-in" or whatever intangible thing makes it feel like human spirits all moving in the same direction. Not enough by half. I don't know what other options we have at this point. It's this or nothing. It's this or death.

When Jesus preached his first sermon, who was there to hear? Did he just start speaking into the noise of the day, send his words out into the air without any crowd to hear? I would have waited for crowds and resources and "momentum" before I began. Did Jesus have to just start telling stories, describing a Kingdom no one had ever imagined, and hope that someone would stop and listen?

I've chosen to override my natural hesitations so often that I don't know anymore when my hesitation is reasonable. I'm praying; I'm discerning with wise people. They're agreeing with me—this is a crazy beyond our usual crazy. Is it my job to throw myself in with abandon?

Is God just asking me to trust? Not to trust what he will do but just to trust that he exists? That he's good? Not to trust that he will make it all work out fine. But to trust that no matter what happens, if I fall flat on my face, if we're all disappointed, if it turns out to be a waste of our time, money, energy, that even that is okay? Is God asking me to leap without expectations of how I'll land? To have no concern for the pain of hitting hard ground? Is it better to risk it all from one big, colossal mess of a gamble than to lose it all slowly because we never risked anything new?

God fed the multitude with a little boy's lunch. He didn't begin with nothing.

He made the wine from water, not from thin air.

But I know that the earlier miracle was the making of the fish, the grain, the water. Even what the disciples offered for God to begin these miracles were miracles he'd already made.

Father,

If this is just not a good use of our time and energy, let us know. But if it's what you're asking us to do, give me courage to speak it into the empty air.

May it land on a few ears, may it turn a few heads, may others catch the vision to reflect to me things I'm saying but don't yet believe. One day, may people I don't yet even know talk with wonder about this thing they're part of that now doesn't yet exist. One day, may I marvel with those who began it with me, may we look at one another and remember how little we had, how much we risked, and may we laugh to retell our surprise at the things you did.

Amen.

"Suppose God tells you to do something that is an enormous test of your common sense, totally going against it. What will you do? Will you hold back? . . .

"By the test of common sense, Jesus Christ's statements may seem mad, but when you test them by the trial of faith, your findings will fill your spirit with the awesome fact that they are the very words of God. Trust completely in God, and when He brings you to a new opportunity of adventure, offering it to you, see that you take it."[3]

OSWALD CHAMBERS

Write Your Own Confession

1. How are you feeling called to do things beyond your own reason?

2. How are you feeling stretched beyond your comfort?

3. Confess your fear and disbelief and temptation not to step in.

4. Confess your desire to follow, your choice to believe, your tentative first steps.

INDIGNANT

How dare he?
He's afraid.
When will he . . . ?
I love him.
Change him.
Change how you see him.

I don't like the way God answers my prayers.

Through the mouth of Jesus, God said people were like "white-washed tombs," called them a "brood of vipers" (Matthew 12:34; 23:27, NIV). And through the prophets he had even harsher language for his people.

And at the same time, on the cross, Jesus said, "Father, forgive them, for they don't know what they are doing" (Luke 23:34). I don't know the difference. When to challenge, when to have compassion? I get the feeling that Jesus' words of challenge were never just to vent or protect himself but in hopes that people would return to God. Guardrails, rumble strips, keeping them from a greater danger.

I don't usually have any interest in being a rumble strip to protect the safety of the person who has wronged me. I just want to protect myself from them. Because this person didn't think before he spoke, now I have to spend hours in prayer, thinking before I speak.

God,
If there is a way you want him to grow from seeing the harm he's done, may I let him see the harm. But not for my own sake.
If there is a way you want me to keep the harm to myself this time, to let it die in me, to teach me your kind of death, let it be.
Amen.

"It does not take long before those in the ministry . . . soon discover they feel like they have been nibbled to death by ducks."[4]

STANLEY HAUERWAS

Write Your Own Confession

1. How do you feel indignant?

2. Confess your desire to force the situation you'd prefer.

3. How can you choose to believe that God can be the source of what you actually need (even if you don't fully feel or understand that belief)?

INSTITUTIONAL

Today we had a newcomer's brunch, a gathering we host several times a year to share about who we are and what we believe as a congregation and to let newcomers ask any questions they have about the church. It's a great way for people to feel welcomed and connected to our mission. And, if I'm honest, it's also a great way to invite them into the system.

It's part of my job. I like the opportunity to help people grow in relationships, of course. I also like the opportunity to get them on the books so we know who's here, who's engaged.

It's a funny thing to lead an institution that's also a family. Today's sermon was from Galatians 3–4—we've been adopted into God's family, are no longer slaves but children and heirs of God's promise. No matter what congregation or denomination (or even with no congregation or denomination), we can be drawn into this promise of welcome in God's family.

God allows this family to have local expressions with actual people, gathering in an actual place. Or else the family would just be a concept. The welcome would be an abstraction. So the local community is meaningful.

And at the same time, it's an organization that pays my wage. And this local community also has bills to pay, a building to upkeep. If the members of this local expression of the family of God don't give in a particular way, we can no longer be this particular expression of God's family. We have regulations and bylaws and a council and a denomination with codes of ethics and best practices. I have to know about all those realities and navigate them and manage them and steward them. And at the same time, this is a family.

The newcomer brunch began when I'd just finished wrapping up the worship service, so I just said, "While we're eating, let's take some time to go around the table. Share your name and a brief description of your previous experience with church, even if you've had none or it's been a negative experience." So between mouthfuls of French toast we heard about various denominational affiliations and family histories. But before long this gathering to invite people to engage with this institution took on an entirely different feel.

There was the story of leaving a cult; there were tears as someone remembered the loss of the parent who had best modeled faith. The tears almost seemed contagious. Now a story of transformation from a life of crime, then a description of illness, now sharing about mental health. All were heartfelt stories of places where God had met these newcomers and made a difference.

We were no longer talking about experiences of church but experiences of God.

We didn't get around to handing out the membership forms.

But we did hand around the box of tissues.

God,
I have a job to oversee this congregation, to keep this
church thriving, to manage the details.
Help me also remember how to talk about you.
Thank you for sending me people who don't know about
the institutional stuff.
Who only know how to talk about the God stuff.
Let me learn from them.
Even as I do the institutional stuff.
Amen.

"Down through the annals of church history, under the pressure of keeping the church going, time and again we Christians have lost the call to be God's faithful presence in the world."[5]

DAVID FITCH

Write Your Own Confession

1. How do you feel the tension between leading an institution and building a relational, missional community?

2. How does it tempt you toward self-sufficiency?

3. How do you choose to trust God instead, even if you're not feeling it yet?

CHAPTER THREE

I WANT TO FORCE MIRACLES

Tremble, earth, at the presence of the Lord, . . .
who turned the rock into a pool,
   the hard rock into springs of water.

PSALM 114:7-8, NIV

How does it feel to be the conduit for a miracle? Moses knew.

God likes to do big, remarkable things through small people. He could have just turned the Nile to blood, just made the sea part. But instead he asked a person to stand there and do something small and seemingly insignificant with a stick. It made the miracle even more surprising. It allowed human eyes to see an agent of the change—an ordinary human with an ordinary stick seemed to begin an obvious cause and effect. Something happened right when that guy did that thing. But the magnitude of the change made no sense in light of the smallness of that person and that stick. So there must have been something else to explain the outcome. When there's a gaping space between the power of the person and the terrifying scale of the miracle, we are left whispering, "Mystery!"

After forty years wandering in the desert, Moses has become accustomed to this pattern: the people grumble, Moses asks God, "What am I to do with these people?" (e.g., Exodus 17:4, NIV) and God asks Moses to do something with that stick again. Forty years before, the complaint had been about water: "Why did you bring us up out of Egypt to make us and our children and livestock die of thirst?" (Exodus 17:3, NIV), and now here is the same complaint in the same dry place, from the same dry mouths: "Why did you bring the LORD's community into this wilderness, that we and our livestock should die here?" (Numbers 20:4, NIV). Forty years prior, God had answered, "Take in your hand the staff with which you struck the Nile. . . . Strike the rock, and water will come out of it for the people to drink" (Exodus 17:5-6, NIV). And now his answer is similar: "Take the staff. . . . Speak to that rock before their eyes and it will pour out its water" (Numbers 20:8, NIV).

This second time, God tells him to take the staff again, so maybe after that Moses stops listening, missing the direction to speak, not hit. He's been doing this for years now. He remembers that the staff has often been the agent of miracles. So once more Moses takes the staff; once more he hits the rock. Two times for good measure. And the water flows.

God does the miracle he promised, but he isn't happy. He's so unhappy with Moses and Aaron that he declares, "Because you did not trust in me enough to honor me as holy in the sight of the Israelites, you will not bring this community into the land I give them" (Numbers 20:12, NIV). It may seem petty to us—the instructions last time were to hit the rock. Moses knew that would work, why not do it again? Wasn't hitting the rock also an act of faith?

It's easy to resent God in stories like this. Come on, God. These guys are old now. They're tired. They've been faithful for so long—let them see the Promised Land. But I must choose to trust God's assessment over my own. God knows what the difference between hitting the rock and speaking to it signifies for Moses. And I daresay Moses knew it too. Is it because Moses is just fed up with the people (he's just said, "Listen, you rebels!" [Numbers 20:10]) and hits the rock out of frustration? Is it because Moses seems to take the credit by saying, "Must we bring you water out of this rock?" (Numbers 20:10, NIV). Is it because he wasn't really listening to God's direction but instead was functioning on autopilot, hitting when he should have been speaking? Is it because words don't break stones but sticks might? Is it that God knew that, after years

of miracles with this staff, Moses had come to think the staff itself was the source of power, like some kind of magic wand? And had Moses confused his possession of that staff with his possession of the power it seemed to wield? Whatever the reason for God's displeasure, it seems to have something to do with Moses' forgetfulness about the source of the miracle.

I've seen a few miracles. I've even watched God use my prayers to work them. So it's tempting for me to demand them again. If I've hit a rock once and the water gushed forth in the desert, I want to go around hitting rocks everywhere I go. Sometimes it's a sign of my belief that God can still do miracles; sometimes it's a sign that I want them to happen in my way and my timing. Often it's a sign that I think the power was in my words.

I do believe that God is powerful. Why are we not seeing miracles today? His Spirit is still active. His Word is still true. Sometimes I look for miracles because I believe. And sometimes I try to force them because I don't.

Thankfully, even when we hit rocks instead of speaking to them, sometimes God does the miracle anyway.

A WITNESS

I thought I'd imagined it. *You've just heard stories about this kind of transformation, hoped for it so much that you've imagined it, Mandy.* But when others commented on it, I knew it wasn't in my mind.

Her eyes are new. Her face is new.

I remember when we met. Her stories gave me nightmares. And every week when we met, she told me more. I think now she wasn't just sharing her stories. She was purging. Poison was leaving her body with every word. Now that it's out of her, she wonders why it had such power over her. Those toxins that once tainted her life now feel innocuous, released by prayer—weeks and weeks of prayer.

And now, now that I look at her face, I see that it's new. I didn't know what was lacking in it until I saw it like this. I would have said before that her face was pleasant, her smile sweet. It's not until you hold fresh flowers that you wonder why the silk ever fooled you into thinking it was real. There's something of sap in you now, Rosie.[1] We all see it.

"How can I proclaim God's liberating Word when no proof will protect me? On the other hand, how can I *not*?

"How can I *not* say it, when I really saw it—God, moving in text and life?"[2]

ANNA CARTER FLORENCE

Father,

Thank you that I get to have a front-row seat to the mysteries.

No, front row implies a distance I don't feel.

Thank you that I get drawn into the play of your mysteries,

get to watch behind the scenes and know when the drama reaches its crescendo just how hard-won it's been.

I remember the drizzly day when I first got the call from Rosie.

I didn't know what she wanted or if I could spare the time for a meeting.

Would it be worth my time?

Thank you for letting me say yes before I knew what you'd do.

Thank you for letting me say yes so now I can say, "I was there when it happened."

I find it hard to confess how much I love these moments.

They're so few and far between.

I don't want to hope for more of them or be disappointed in waiting for the next one.

But let me be restored by them as they come, not keep them at arm's length.

I'd rather live looking and hoping for them and be discouraged when they're hard to see than harden my heart and miss them.

Let me be an unflinching witness. Wake me up so I don't miss a moment.

Amen.

Write Your Own Confession

1. Even if it's been a while since it happened, remember a time you saw someone made new. (Maybe it was you.)

2. Let yourself remember how they were before and after. (Even if the miracle was not instantaneous, slow miracles are still miracles. Going from dark to light, from death to life, is always a miracle.)

3. How can you celebrate the miracles around you and within you?

4. How can you set aside the desire to be safe and let yourself risk miracles?

5. Confess the ways you long for miracles.

DELUSIONAL

I saw the headline last week that a large, wealthy congregation split from its denomination. And the headline the week before about Christians publicly making outrageous claims in Jesus' name. This week there are two news stories about Christian leaders abusing power and being asked to step down, leaving their organizations in a tailspin (two more to add to a long list). And this morning before church I heard the whispers about several key members being upset about changes in the congregation. I heard about the heated discussion in the hallway after church between two people with very different perspectives on sexuality.

My own body is woven into a global Body that's in a paroxysm. The spasming across denominations and congregations is felt by us all. When I pay attention, I'm aware of a subtle kind of trauma, like someone has shaken me, hard. And although a good shaking doesn't leave you bruised, it sets up a persistent tremor in places no one can see. If we're honest, we'll admit we all feel the shaking.

And still it's our role to represent this disrupted and disrupting Body. This week there's still a sermon to be written, a Bible study to be prepared, and a church retreat to be planned. It's still my job to cast vision for what a church (the church?) can be, even as I'm traumatized by what the church can be. As I plan this retreat, I read Dietrich Bonhoeffer's *Life Together*, hoping for help casting a vision of Christian community for this little congregation, daring to imagine—together—that we can be transformed into the likeness of Christ, even more so because we're together.

But within the first four sentences, Bonhoeffer confronts me with this: "Jesus Christ lived in the midst of his enemies. At the end all his disciples deserted him. On the Cross he was utterly alone, surrounded by evildoers and mockers."[3] Before I've finished the first page, my anxieties rise to the surface in tears. I lament that this was the case for Jesus and that it's the case for all who follow him. We are drawn into Christian community because of all it promises. The joy of what we hope it can be leads us into pain after pain after pain.

I close the book around my pencil and set it aside (my tears have long since blurred the words) to ask the Lord, *Why does this thing that you promise will be the hope of the world so often break our hearts? How can I keep hoping for it to be what I hope it can be? How can I keep proclaiming this promise to people when I'm still waiting to see it?* I know that the proclamation of what church can be helps it become what it can be. I know what it can be even though I've only experienced it in snatches. Hope is a discipline. I choose it today.

> *God,*
>> *I know you see all the brokenness I see in your church.*
>> *You see it and more.*
>> *I know your heart breaks more than mine does.*
>> *You love the church more than I do.*
>> *I know that this is not the first time your church has been through upheaval.*
>> *I know you are not surprised, not anxious, not despairing.*
>> *I know that even as you grieve you have a greater joy.*
>> *The story would be a tragedy if it finished here.*
>> *But it's not yet finished.*
>> *Give me faith to see what you see, all the possibilities hidden in the brokenness.*
>> *Give me courage to proclaim it even though it makes me sound delusional.*
>> *Give me hope that makes no human sense.*
>> *May I trust that the tiny seeds in your Body can still spring into life.*
>> *May I trust in the power of compost, the life that comes from all that's dying.*
>> *When I see only seeds, may I speak of gardens.*
>> *Amen.*

"Hope is optimism with a broken heart."[4]

Write Your Own Confession

1. How do you avoid letting yourself hope?

2. How does it keep you from proclaiming things you can't see?

3. Confess how your preferred outcomes separate you from God.

DISAPPOINTED.

He's back in rehab. I went away for two weeks, and he's back in rehab. His story had been one of hope, the whole congregation watching the transformation in his life, asking one another, "Remember how he was when he first came? Remember how he looked, how he spoke?" He'd seen darkness and despair, and something about Jesus got his attention, shook him hard, woke him up to light and life. And he hasn't looked back.

Until now.

I've just arrived home from a trip. Before I left, I asked folks to check in with him. I wrote him notes of encouragement to be sent in my absence. And then I left. I left because I needed a break and because I trusted that ultimately I am not the source of his hope. But upon arriving home, I hear that he went into rehab just a few days after I left. I can't help feeling I shouldn't have traveled. Of course I should have. But what might have happened if I hadn't?

He'd been doing so well these past months. He'd been telling his story of recovery from addiction. We'd been feeling our own faith confirmed. We'd chosen to trust in miracles. The whole congregation has been happy for him and for us—could this truly be a place where lives can be changed? Could the same transformation be possible in us? Does healing still literally happen? We've been praying for it and seeing signs of it. But now a relapse.

I'm disappointed for him.

And if I'm honest, I'm also disappointed for me. And for us.

The obvious work of the Spirit in him was lifting my own wounded heart, making me feel like this work is worth it. If I'm honest, some small part of me feels like his relapse reflects poorly on my capability. Will the congregation lose heart? Lose faith in me and the big claims I choose to make, albeit with trembling lips?

Hope is tender. Can it outlive disappointment?

I'm still getting over jet lag. I wasn't planning to go back to work for two more days. I'm worried about him. Should I call and check on him? What difference does two days make? Ultimately he is in God's hands. But sometimes God sends humans to show his love. Is it God's love I hope to share with him? Or am I seeking something in that encounter—some sense of my own capacity to fix people—that will comfort me? Am I willing to step into the mess of wherever he is for his sake? Or do I want to resolve it to relieve the pain of my own failure and disappointment?

Lord,

   What kind of torment drives a human soul to seek a kind of quick relief that slowly kills them? Lord, have mercy on all trapped in addiction.

   And release me from the kind of quick relief I also seek.

   What kind of life is this that just the act of living slowly drains us? Christ, have mercy.

   What will save us from this body of death?

   I can't bear my own pain, much less the pain of others.

   I long to see true, unshakable transformation.

   I long to see your Kingdom come on earth as it is in heaven.

   I see glimpses, but they're never enough, hints passing in a cloudy mirror.

   I want to force your Kingdom here, now.

   We need your face. Unadulterated, unsubtle. Not hints and hopes but actual, unquestionable presence. Eye to eye.

   Come, Lord Jesus!

Write Your Own Confession

1. How do you want to save others? How do you want to save yourself?

2. Confess the quick relief you seek when you feel yourself sinking.

3. How is God inviting you once more to choose him over all the things that promise relief?

4. Confess that belief, even if your hand still reaches for something else as you say the words.

FAR FROM GOD

How did I get myself here? To this place where it's so hard to find signs of God? Where is he? I thought it was God leading me here. So why did following God not lead me to more of God?

I remember now.

We were on a walk in the woods. Just me and God.

He felt so apparent, so that even with the slightest breeze he got my attention. The green was somehow greener than I'd ever noticed. And although I didn't hear the words from God I longed to hear, he had something deeper for me. All the beauty of the world seemed, at least for a moment, to be just for me. We were just together in it. And it was everything.

And from those blessed days in those woods, I heard God drawing me toward something. Which felt to me like a promise of more of God. How could I say no? I said yes because I wanted to live in that state of blessed presence every single moment. But now, two years later, all the little yeses that I said on that day and that I've said since have led me to a place that feels very little like the place where it all began.

I have to work very hard to calm myself long enough to find God's presence, and even then, I wonder if I'm imagining it. How did my yes from that place of presence lead me to this place of absence? Did I get it wrong? Was that really God back there in the woods? Or did I misunderstand what he was asking me to move toward?

I just wanted to receive more of God. But was God asking me to be a missionary to bring more of him? Did God take me from his presence, or did he put me in a place where his presence is not known so that I can say, "Look! Here is God, already here among us!"? Is the power of that presence from two years ago in those woods supposed to sustain me in what feels like a desert? I'm tempted to just return to those woods. But I have a feeling I could not enter back into that moment. Is the joy of those woods and the longing for them my prompt to drop to my knees and dig right here, in this hard ground, to find tiny shoots of the woods beginning to emerge in unseen places right under our feet?

God,
I want your presence and I want you to reveal it.
I want you to do the work of making yourself known.
In some places it's harder to see you.
Someone must start saying, "God is already here!"
I don't want to be that person.
I want your presence obvious already, to join what you're already up to.
Help me bring the joy I've seen to people who've never seen it, to not resent them for not knowing the joys I've known.
Stir whatever you've planted in me. Don't let it die in the desert.
Give me what I need to dig and dig and dig and invite others into the digging, for the joy of what we don't yet see.
Amen.

"To say day by day 'Thy Kingdom Come' . . . does not mean: 'I quite hope that some day the Kingdom of God will be established. . . . But at present I don't see how it is to be managed or what I can do about it.' On the contrary, it means, or should mean, 'Here am I! Send me!'—active, costly collaboration with the Spirit in whom we believe."[5]

EVELYN UNDERHILL

Write Your Own Confession

1. How do you feel your obedience to God has led you to a place that feels far from God?

2. Write your confession of what you're tempted to do to resolve that oxymoron.

3. What if that original calling has not been forgotten?

4. How can you (genuinely) confess something that looks like belief in the bitterness?

IMMERSED

All the baptisms I've done before have been in a portable baptistry. A big bath in a big box on wheels. So I've stood, safe and dry on the floor, leaning over the person getting wet. But today it's a pool. A public pool at that. So I wade into the water, waist-deep. I wade in first. What kind of job is this that requires the whole self? To get soaked, drenched. Immersed. Fully.

Later that night, as I look at the photos of the day, one particularly strikes me. It shows me just doing my job, drawing up Bernie from the water. But on a gut level, I know it's not a photo of me helping a grown man up from some chlorinated water. What I'm holding in that photo is a newborn. It feels weird to name it. I didn't feel it at the time. I don't really want to think of this grown man as a baby. He's older than me. I didn't give birth to him. Nevertheless he looks newly born, and the way I'm holding him seems somehow like he's fresh and needing someone to catch him. And my face. I have the face a human has when encountering pure, miraculous new life.

Midwives get to be there every day, immersed in the messy moment of life beginning. I have to wait months, often years, for the next opportunity to witness this kind of birth, to have the joy of guiding a new life into the world, somehow.

I look again at my face, captured in that moment of catching up that large, slippery newborn, awkward and self-conscious as he was. And I know I was born for this. All the frustration of my daily work, all the disappointments, all the emails with roofers, and meetings about fundraising all happen so that once or twice a year I get to do this.

Lord, thank you for the joy of being part of new life,
   right in the center of the story with someone feeling fresh and frail,
   immersed with them in the mysteries and coming up to newness of life.
   Each time, may I remember why I said yes to this call.
   Each time, may I remember why I'm so often feeling dropped in the deep end.
   Give me capacity for these times.
   Give me capacity for the long times between these times.
   Amen.

"There was a young couple strolling along half a block ahead of me. The sun had come up brilliantly after a heavy rain, and the trees were glistening and very wet. On some impulse, plain exuberance, I suppose, the fellow jumped up and caught hold of a branch, and a storm of luminous water came pouring down on the two of them, and they laughed and took off running. . . . It was a beautiful thing to see, like something from a myth. . . . [It] is easy to believe in such moments that water was made primarily for blessing."[6]

MARILYNNE ROBINSON

Write Your Own Confession

1.   What gives you capacity to receive joy in your work when it comes? And what gives you capacity to wait for the joy when it doesn't come?

2.   Confess your choice to join God in the place where ordinary life encounters the extraordinary.

3.   Confess however you need him to give you capacity for it.

RELYING . . . EVEN IN ABUNDANCE

For months I waited. I begged God to move, to do something here that might save a church. I wondered if he heard me, but I kept waiting, watching the hard ground for any sign of life. I don't know how to garden in desert places. Is it even wise?

Am I just imagining it, or am I seeing tiny new shoots spring up? I only kept waiting, hoping, proclaiming the possibilities because I had some belief he could do it. And now that belief has become *of course*. Of course God could do this; he has done bigger miracles before.

I said thanks to God just one time and then moved on into this new landscape where new life is normal. I miss the way the desperate waiting drew me to God every morning, drove me to ask, to turn to him, to remember the source of life—my own and this church's.

How can this gratitude lead me to God as much as the waiting did? How can abundance turn my face to him as often as scarcity did? I don't need as much imagination anymore to see that God is here. How did his obvious action become an opportunity to stop talking to him? When did I start to cruise? To feel entitled? It's good to have a break from desperation. No one can live there forever. But when the relief comes, I want to remember my need for God, even in plenty.

My God, what does it look like to know my reliance when I feel competent?
I could not proclaim a thing without the lungs you formed.
This little heart could not care unless you had first loved me.
May every blessing become an opportunity for praise.
May every provision remind me I have nothing without you.
Amen.

"You made us with yourself as our goal, and our heart is restless until it rests in you."[7]

AUGUSTINE

Write Your Own Confession

1. How do you feel competent? How do you have what you need?

2. Confess how it makes you independent, how you take the credit.

3. Write a confession of your desire to find your needs met in God, even if you don't always feel them.

_____

_____

_____

_____

_____

_____

_____

_____

_____

_____

_____

_____

_____

CHAPTER FOUR

I WANT TO KNOW OUTCOMES

Indeed, [he] has found the way, for he has said: "I do not know."

QUOTED IN *THE SAYINGS OF THE DESERT FATHERS*,

TRANS. BENEDICTA WARD

The book of Job is strewn with question marks, small signs a tiny serpent has been this way. Stumbling in the darkness to find answers to his suffering, Job hopes the next step might bring him to the satisfying solid ground of a full stop. But instead his foot finds another question, a moving muscle of serpent that sends him sliding, sliding. Kicking for a foothold only awakens more slithery questions. And we feel ourselves slipping with Job as he cries:

> "Why did I not die at birth . . . ?"
>
> JOB 3:11, NRSV

> "Why is light given to one in misery,
>   and life to the bitter in soul . . . ?"
>
> JOB 3:20, NRSV

> "What are human beings, that you make so much of them,
>   that you set your mind on them,
> visit them every morning,
>   test them every moment? . . .
> If I sin, what do I do to you, you watcher of humanity?

69

Why have you made me your target?
Why have I become a burden to you?"

JOB 7:17-18, 20, NRSV

Will Job's life ever amount to more than questions? Will there ever be a satisfying resolution to his story? The pain of lost certainty is as excruciating as the pain of lost loves and livestock!

But amid all he demands of the darkness and all the arguments he has with himself, it's in the moments of greatest absurdity that Job becomes most sane. When every question only brings more questions and his hunger for answers is most ravenous, Job arrives, panting, at the end of himself. And finally, for just a moment, Job pauses from his thrashing to take a breath. And now, here, from a point of stillness in the very center of the torment, we hear a surprising groundedness:

"But where shall wisdom be found?
    And where is the place of understanding?
Mortals do not know the way to it,
    and it is not found in the land of the living.
The deep says, 'It is not in me,'
    and the sea says, 'It is not with me.' . . .
Where then does wisdom come from? . . .
God understands the way to it,
    and he knows its place."

JOB 28:12-14, 20, 23, NRSV

With all Job has lost, something has not left him. In the depth of deepest dark, there is an ember in him that will not be extinguished. Beyond all his unfilled answer-hunger there is a greater hunger—for the living God. What does it cost Job—in this place where God's goodness seems inconceivable—to proclaim these words?

"I know that my Redeemer lives,
    and that at the last he will stand upon the earth;

and after my skin has been thus destroyed,
> then in my flesh I shall see God,
whom I shall see on my side,
> and my eyes shall behold, and not another.
> My heart faints within me!"

JOB 19:25-27, NRSV

At last Job will have his God-hunger met. When all has been said and still there is no reasonable explanation for Job's desperate state, God himself appears like a whirlwind. God does not minimize the terror of unknowing. To end the conversation, God does not give answers.

To end the conversation, God asks bigger questions:

> "Where were you when I laid the foundation of the earth? . . .
> > Who laid its cornerstone
> when the morning stars sang together
> > and all the heavenly beings shouted for joy?"

JOB 38:4, 6-7, NRSV

At last Job's true answer has come because Job's God has come.

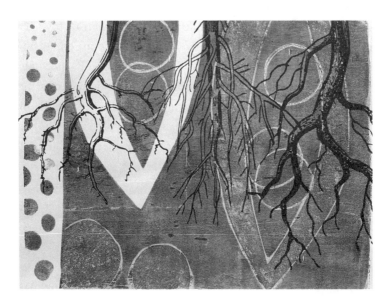

JUST TIRED

I'm just old-fashioned, plain old tired.

And to make it worse, I feel a bit guilty for feeling tired.

I know that since God is powerful, he can take our small efforts and make them more than they are. Through a small boy he kills a giant, with one lunch he feeds thousands, and he fills clay vessels with the glory of the universe. So if I truly trust in the power of God and his capacity to embody it in human lives—two realities proclaimed by the very body of Jesus—I will just keep plodding along, and he will somehow make me able to do what needs to be done.

But there's a grief that's sapping my batteries, even when I'm not conscious of it. It finds me waking with tears already pooling in my closed eyes before I'm even aware of the sadness. In every crowd I see the person I'm missing, even when I'm not aware I'm looking for him. Is it possible to be haunted by the ghost of someone who, as far as I know, is still alive?

And there's something about my work that's keeping me from doing the things that give me life. It's a normal part of ministry to have to do things that you're not good at and don't enjoy. But something dies when that's most of our work. And it's not only something in us that dies. The things we should and could be doing that grow from our joy also die, withering in that distant land of undone things. Songs unsung.

But even in my faith that you can use me, small and tired as I am, is there something about my pushing on through the tiredness that is not faithful?

Are there ways that you can be good even if these things don't get done? Even if someone else does them or I do them some other time? Are there miracles you want to do when I'm doing nothing, which I may never see until I stop?

I don't even know how to do that. It all feels pressing and

essential. If I'm honest, I feel like I'm just doing the bare minimum (and at the same time, that it's never enough).

I don't make good decisions when I'm tired. Especially decisions about rest.

Today I had a meeting at the end of the day. Why did I set this meeting for the end of the day when my energy is gone? I knew it was a mistake when I left the house disgruntled. The resentment turned to a kind of panic as I hit afternoon traffic. What was I thinking, setting a meeting on the other side of the city at peak hour? But a foreign idea came to me: *You could call and ask to meet by phone this time.* Is that allowed? Does that look unprofessional? Does it communicate that I don't care about this person or the reason for our meeting? It felt strangely wrong but also freeing to pull out of traffic and call to ask if we could talk by phone. The voice on the other end was unflapped by the change. A tiny possibility into a different life opened up—what else am I doing that doesn't really need to be done?

God,

I confess I need your help to even see where I can stop.

I confess I need your guidance to show me when things don't really need to be done.

I need you to show me the moments when I'm pushing through when I should be giving up.

I need you to show me the people I can ask to take on something for me.

I need you to show me how they might be blessed to see I'm human, how they might be blessed to be asked to help.

I do trust you can use this tired body and mind to show your strength.

I even trust that you can show your strength when my tired body and mind are doing nothing at all. Maybe especially then.

Amen.

> "I am a frayed and nibbled survivor in a fallen world,
> and I am getting along."[1]

ANNIE DILLARD

Write Your Own Confession

1. How are you tired? How does it draw you away from God?

2. Confess your preferences for self-reliance.

3. How does the tiredness hold invitations to need God again?

4. Write a confession of dependence in the tiredness.

ANTICIPATING

I wrote these confessions as journal entries, opening a blank document and letting my fingers try to do something on the keyboard that could keep up with my racing mind and flooded heart. When I click to open one called "Anticipating," the document is blank. Which seems fitting.

Write Your Own Confession

1. In what area of your life do you find yourself most in anticipation? What are you anticipating? How does it affect your relationship with God?

2. How can you confess any way you're tempted to turn from God in your anticipation?

3. How can you confess once more a choice to trust in God more than in resolution?

LOST IN THE LAND OF "AS LONG AS . . ."

When I was commissioned for this role, I told you I'd join you here, Lord.

That you'd already been working here long before me in this place and these people.

My appearance here was not the beginning of your work but the next season of it.

I knew this is ultimately your work, your church.

But on a daily basis, it's (also) my work.

And there are a lot of things that need to be done, not only for the sake of to-do lists and compliance and all those sensible things. They need to be done for the sake of survival. When numbers (of dollars and people) and hope are small, the daily decisions we make, of how we use our time, are vital. Literally vital—they can be deciding factors in whether we live.

That's a lot to carry every day, Lord.

Why have you given me so much to carry?

As long as I never make any mistakes,

As long as I don't upset anyone,

As long as we don't have a major repair bill . . .

We'll be okay.

Will we be okay?

I'm lost in the land of "as long as . . ." There's no grace here. But there's a lot of anxiety.

Everything I do feels weighty, directly connected to the life or death of a community.

I do believe that God is ultimately overseeing all things, that this is his church, not mine. At the same time, I know he's given us agency. I've seen how one person's decisions can do serious damage to the work of God. I've watched one person's leadership split an entire community.

There's something about the birth of a child that makes you want to take them to your favorite places, even though you know they won't remember them. When our daughter was a month old, we took a ferry across a river to the apple orchards. Usually I'd get out of the car, stand by the railing, and watch the water. But now the new weight of parenthood opened a dreadful part of my imagination that visualized the power I had to inadvertently harm this tiny person whose life was in my hands. On this ferry I could only imagine myself dropping my newborn over into the cold depths and her sinking, sinking. So we sat in the car until safely on dry land again. Of course, I would never choose to drop a child into a river, but as a new mother, the weight of my agency, the possibility that I could physically do it was more than I could bear. I was new to parenthood and to the fear that my own power could ruin someone else. I never outgrew that dread; I just got used to it.

The same is true in ministry. My own weaknesses, stupidity, carelessness could, within just one day, do great damage to this place. So I make choices carefully. I weigh my words.

Feeling reverence for this work is healthy. But God never called me to make sure nothing bad ever happens. That didn't seem to be Jesus' call, either. In fact, he seemed to create chaos wherever he went. He said what he liked, went where the Spirit led. He wasn't trying to keep a little church alive.

I can't live in this land of "as long as . . ."

I'm done with the lie *We'll be okay as long as the church never splits or has to close, as long as we never run out money* and the lie *I'll be okay as long as my loved ones never leave, my health never fails, and we never face war or other crises.*

That kind of life is a death before death, the carrying of a weight we were never asked to bear.

But the eternal life we've been promised is on the other side of the right kind of death.

I'm dying to all the things that will die.

I don't want painful things to happen to anyone in this little community.

I want this place to keep worshiping and serving here.
I don't want to fail or disappoint anyone.
But churches do run out of money and people.
Congregations do close.
Pastors do make mistakes.

As far as I know, not one of the original first-century congregations still exists. But what a thing they began! Jesus promised he'd build his church. But not this particular congregation.

There's a strange freedom in letting my imagination go there. If we closed, we would grieve. All these people and resources would go to other places. And they'd keep serving and worshiping there.

Father,
> *I release all that's here.*
> *These people, these buildings, these hymnbooks and pew Bibles, this Communion table and piano. Everything in our bank account.*
> *Our history and our hopes for the future.*
> *I release them all to you.*
> *May they be fully used for your Kingdom, wherever that is.*
> *I'd like it to be here. But even if it's not, we'll be okay.*
> *We lose our life to find it.*
> *Amen.*

"The old life is left behind, and completely surrendered. The disciple is dragged out of . . . relative security into a life of absolute insecurity, from a life which is observable and calculable into a life where everything is unobservable and fortuitous, out of the realm of finite, and into the realm of infinite possibilities. Once again, the new life is not a law, not a set of principles, a programme, or an ideal. Discipleship means Jesus Christ, and Him alone. It cannot consist of anything more than that."[2]

DIETRICH BONHOEFFER

Write Your Own Confession

1. How are you living in the land of "as long as . . ."? How does it undercut grace?

2. Confess any way that anxiety leads to the practical atheism of self-sufficiency.

3. How could you let yourself imagine losing all the things you think you need?

4. How, in that place, might you have a deeper sense of need for God?

5. How might you confess that need now?

MAKING NO SENSE

I can empathize with people who don't understand why I'm doing what I'm doing.

It's not like I'm comfortable with it either. You ask me to explain? Is *God told me to* enough of a reason? It's barely enough for me, so why should I imagine it's enough for you? I dare not admit to them how vague the "telling" is.

When I'm stretched beyond my comfort, when I'm saying yes to things I can't explain, how can I possibly explain them to anyone else? Some of these prompts I may never understand. Some of them will never have obvious fruit (unless you count the stretching of our faith). But one thing I do know—we won't have a hope of learning what God's doing unless we say yes to his promptings. And then, sometimes, new things come about that couldn't have if we'd waited to understand before acting. While not every risk pays off, everything that's fruitful can be traced back to a risk. My favorite people are the ones who are willing to take risks with me.

The hardest people to lead are those who create this maddening situation: I feel led in a particular direction and I know that if we, as a community, move in that direction, together we'll come to understand it. But there's always a few who plant their feet and demand an explanation before joining. We get into a stalemate as they say, "I'm not coming along until I understand" and I say, "We won't understand until you come along."

I'm not trying to be difficult, honestly. I'm frustrated with the vagueness too!

It might alleviate some of the frustration if I could say, "I hear you. I'm confused by God's direction too!" But claiming God's direction has been abused for too long by leaders. And for folks who plant their feet until they can be convinced, there's only one thing more annoying than a lack of explanation from their leader:

an explanation that blames God for the confusion. I wish I could tell them how much I need to watch their following of God to understand what he's doing here. Perhaps then I could explain to them why they should follow.

Father,
> *Give me enough direction to know how to begin.*
> *What is the next step?*
> *And give me enough friends for the journey to move ahead.*
> *Who are you sending to journey with me?*
> *May those who plant their feet begin to see something.*
> *I don't move ahead to leave them behind, but to begin the thing that will help them understand enough to want to join in.*
> *Don't let me leave them behind.*
> *And in it all, give me courage to move toward things I can't yet see or explain, even to myself.*
> *May we all come to a day when we look at one another, rejoicing in the things we've found together, saying, "I'm so glad we took the risk!"*
> *Amen.*

"I'm a follower of Christ who can't keep up."[3]

BONO

Write Your Own Confession

1. How are you feeling called to do things that make no sense?

2. How does it stretch your faith?

3. Confess your temptation toward your own understanding, toward avoidance of risk.

4. How is this a moment for inviting God's imagination?

5. Write your confession of however you need to see with God's eyes.

UNREQUITED

The skies are clearing after early morning rain as I push open the church's wide doors. A young dad parks illegally for a minute to shuffle his sleepy daughter across the street to school. I can see his mind is already on the day's work.

For me today's work is the first gathering of a new Bible study. When a newcomer asked, "Do you have a Bible study?" I responded, "No, let's start one!" And from that slender start, today we're meeting for the first time to talk about what it might mean to meet.

I'm not sure that even those who said they'll come will come. But I write, "Bible study here. Join us!" on the chalkboard sign, letting myself imagine a crazy possibility—that we could have more people than planned, not less. As I prop the sign on the sidewalk, I feel a flicker of fear. A familiar flicker that I'm learning to endure.

The Bibles are stacked and ready, the chairs arranged, the teapot filled, and there are still minutes before we're due to begin. Surely a few folks would be here by now if they're planning to come? I'm aware of the possibility that in fifteen minutes, maybe twenty, it might become apparent that no one's coming. I see myself tipping the tea down the sink.

For now, I let myself stand in that open doorway and watch the street. The drizzle begins again, melting my chalk invitation, making the passing feet rush even more quickly past my open door. There's a reason this door has been made to swing wide, right on this corner. This aspect of the edifice was made for invitation, and this building has been opening herself to this neighborhood since many years before I came here. How can she endure it? To swing open wide doors with generous vulnerability, letting yourself love and hope, opening yourself to disappointment, rejection. As I watch the puddled street, look at my smeared sign that's gone unseen, I'm aware of a familiar feeling. It takes a minute to name it: the teenage angst of unrequited love. But back then, when the boy was unattainable, at some point you moved on. It's just dumb to keep loving something so unlikely. But to stop loving now would feel like a betrayal.

So I choose to stand and look with longing out on this street. If anyone had time to look up and see me, I'd make a pathetic scene—a lone pastor waiting in the doorway of an old church. I don't want to stand here with my heart and door open; I want to run away. But for as long as I can endure it, I keep standing in the open doorway, watching the traffic pass, the chalk smear. I let myself hope for the thing that's lacking, for the resolution of this tension. Some part of that tension comes from my own desire to see an outcome, to be able to say that my new Bible study drew in crowds. But my longing also grows from today's Bible passage, knowing the transformative work it can do in an earnest heart. I watch that man rushing his daughter to school, those sleepy passengers on that bus, that lady helping kids at the crosswalk. If only they knew how much they're loved.

Musicals have ruined me for normal life. They've taught me to imagine a street full of harried people could suddenly all break into the same song, miraculously moving in time to perfect choreography. My heart wants the passing bus to stop and empty out into my church, joyful faces all singing God's praises, the Friday morning monotony turned, in the blink of an eye, to something otherworldly.

If they all came and heard and received, it would resolve this tension I'm feeling. But that's probably not going to happen today. There's a simpler way I could resolve the tension: I could just stop wishing and hoping. As I stand in that doorway, longer than I can bear (although I'm sure it's only moments), I ask God how I'm supposed to endure this always waiting, always inviting, always risking rejection. And what I sense from God is a melancholy smile. A welcome into his waiting.

Loving God,

It feels like too much to send out invitations to something that doesn't yet exist.

I want to join a thing already in full swing, be part of a movement that has obvious, measurable momentum.

Help me not only open the doors but do so with joy.

Help me swing them wide with abandon.

Even as I fear looking foolish, being rejected, feeling unsuccessful, grow in me a desire for something that's better than all that.

Even as I feel the risk of rejection, I know I've rejected you.

I've left your invitations hanging.

Draw me deeper into your own heart.

Teach me your capacity for welcoming and waiting.

Amen.

"How often I have longed to gather your children together, as a hen gathers her chicks under her wings, and you were not willing."

LUKE 13:34, NIV

Write Your Own Confession

1. Where does your heart go when you invite people who may or may not respond?

2. How does it make you want to flee to a safer place? Confess how it takes you out of connection with God.

3. How is God inviting you to wait and hope with him, vulnerable though it may be?

4. Confess your willingness to shelter in him even in that waiting.

CHAPTER FIVE

I WANT TO FEEL SUCCESSFUL

God doesn't call me to be successful. God calls me to be faithful.
MOTHER TERESA, QUOTED IN JIM TOWEY, *TO LOVE AND BE LOVED*

By the time Paul writes his letters he seems confident of his calling, able to tell a positive story of his imprisonments and sufferings. But I can read between the lines. I get the feeling he's had to do a lot of wrestling with God to overcome the shame. His story could also be described as a disastrous decision to leave behind the accolades and stability of a successful career to take a path of dishonor, persecution, and imprisonment. This scholar who was once lauded as a great protector of the Jewish faith has now become prince of all persecuted. If a painless life is a sign of God's blessing, then he is far from grace. If being unopposed is a sign that your teaching is correct, he's way off track.

I know what success looks like when I see it in others. They seem to know the future and make decisions with clarity. All their plans unfold without a hitch. They swim in a sea of consensus and appreciation. They push forward from strength to strength with no detours. It looks like confidence and popularity and unity and measurable outcomes. It also looks implausible. But delicious. So delicious.

We don't always get to see Paul's wrestling. I want to watch his distress as he learns of the suffering of his children in the faith and feels the feebleness of his prison-cell prayers for them. I want to see his face in the moments when one more friend has betrayed him, when one more follower has abandoned the faith. I wish I could hear the words he whimpers when it's just him and the walls of a dank dungeon, when the God who got him into this mess feels far away. Did Paul feel he had failed?

I imagine he did. The passionate tone of victory in his letters is the tone of turning. It's the sound someone makes when they've been in the depths, fighting the darkness. It's the exertion of the baptized surging up, from death to new life:

> I want to know Christ—yes, to know the power of his resurrection and participation in his sufferings, becoming like him in his death, and so, somehow, attaining to the resurrection from the dead.
>
> PHILIPPIANS 3:10-11, NIV

and

> Who shall separate us from the love of Christ? Shall trouble or hardship or persecution or famine or nakedness or danger or sword? . . .
>
> No, in all these things we are more than conquerors through him who loved us. For I am convinced that neither death nor life, neither angels nor demons, neither the present nor the future, nor any powers, neither height nor depth, nor anything else in all creation, will be able to separate us from the love of God that is in Christ Jesus our Lord.
>
> ROMANS 8:35, 37-39, NIV

and

> We are hard pressed on every side, but not crushed; perplexed, but not in despair; persecuted, but not abandoned; struck down, but not destroyed. We always carry around in our body the death of Jesus, so that the life of Jesus may also be revealed in our body.
>
> 2 CORINTHIANS 4:8-10, NIV

These are not lifeless memory verses but declarations from a suffering servant who refuses to let prison and rejection and loss have the last word. And those words ring through the centuries to find us in what feels like failure.

When I have a public failure, I feel ashamed, but Paul boasts in his imprisonment. When friends and followers walk away, I question my beliefs, but in rejection Paul chooses to stay the course. When obedience takes me to suffering, I'm tempted to feel forsaken by God. But Paul determines to see his suffering as a sign of solidarity with Christ. When ridiculed I want to put up a façade, but Paul gushes about his tears, his longing, his joy. It's not because he's invincible. It's because, like our Lord, he has known the darkness, been tempted in it, and chosen the light. He emerges, not unscathed, but with the tenacity to tell the darkness, "The more you dump on me, the harder I'll dig for light. The more you oppress me, the more I'll treasure the One who refuses to oppress. The more powerful you think you are, the more passion I'll have to preach the good news that in our weakness Christ is strong!"

SWAMPED BY SPREADSHEETS

This week somehow two important meetings fell on the same day—an afternoon vision-casting meeting for leaders across the state and an evening congregational budget meeting. I'd been looking over spreadsheets for this meeting to plan the annual budget, but I still didn't feel ready, so I had the morning blocked out to look at the spreadsheets again. As I planned my day, I noticed that the afternoon meeting is taking place eight minutes from the beach. Why not take my spreadsheets to the beach? If I have to do the work, I might as well do it in a beautiful location.

So I left early, with a spreadsheet printout and highlighter and a big bag of beach clothes and meeting clothes. As I got out of the car, the sea breeze hit me and knocked something out of me: something serious and anxious and overly responsible was just gone. And the idea of looking at a spreadsheet on a beach was suddenly preposterous. I had an instinct (which I can only imagine was from God, because I don't speak to myself with such grace) that said: *What if the best way to prepare for an intense meeting is to spend the morning on the beach?*

It goes against deep lessons from culture, deep fears about productivity, deep understandings of what it means to be responsible, but I need to keep asking, *Could this really be true that resting brings the kind of productiveness we see in plants—their very life becoming fruit?*

Contemplative theologian Thomas Merton said, "The more we persist in misunderstanding the phenomena of life, the more we analyze them out into strange finalities and complex purposes of our own, the more we involve ourselves in sadness, absurdity and despair."[1]

Every morning, when the things that need to be done in the day are weighing on my mind, I choose to walk to the river. I'd rather jump onto email or start the sermon. It would make me feel like I'm getting somewhere. But instead I walk to the river, a long walk down the hill to the shore. And today I realize why. It's a kind of daily baptism, a dying to all the ways I want to tame this day, a rising again to join this day I did not make. Each time I clamber back up the hill from the river to my little office to dive into the day, I find this little reminder scrawled on a card in orange pencil:

> God's foolishness is wiser than human wisdom, and God's weakness is stronger than human strength.
>
> I CORINTHIANS 1:25, NRSV

Somehow this morning baptism brings me back into the day with more energy than all my efforts to have energy. This lowering and rising allows me to leave behind all I'm carrying, and somehow, I'm free.

Father, give me an imagination for the way you work and the way you invite me to work with you.

Stretch me beyond the ingrained habits of thinking and working, and let me keep choosing the discomfort of resting in you, trusting that your Spirit really can work even when I don't feel prepared and that preparing for your work sometimes means doing nothing at all.

Amen.

"Don't be empty air, my soul. Do not let your heart grow hard of hearing in the racket of your emptiness. You, too, must listen: the Word itself shouts for you to return, and there lies a place of calm that will never know any uproar, where love is not abandoned unless it abandons."[2]

AUGUSTINE

Write Your Own Confession

1. How do you feel swamped by details?

2. How does it tempt you toward self-sufficiency? Confess it even if it's messy.

3. What kind of baptism is God inviting you into—what is he asking you to let die? What does he want to come alive?

EXTRAPOLATING

Yesterday was hard. As I lay in bed, the pain was like a poison in my heart, coursing through my veins. Someone I'd relied on just didn't show up. I lay there, limp, a withered plant, leaves drying, curling. After all I've invested in that person, trusting them to step up. Is my work all in vain? The past felt poisoned: *Nothing I've done makes any difference.* And the poison was seeping into the future: *Nothing I do will ever make a difference.* And how can I live with this pain every day? It shrivels my sense of self. I thought my ministry was more compelling, that people were finding true connection to God here. Maybe I'm not called to this.

And I felt drawn, down toward death, dark but strangely delicious: *Yes, I am nothing. I have been and will be nothing.*

Self-pity is surprisingly cozy.

Self-loathing is dangerously sweet.

But then a small, sharp caution:

Don't go there.

The pain, the disappointment, and the sadness are real.

Let yourself feel them in the moment.

Be present to the pain.

But don't extrapolate. Don't let the pain become poison that seeps into your story, drying up your life.

Your disappointment today does not mean that you are a disappointment.

Don't let the darkness tell the story.

God of this moment,

I'm good at telling stories. But people in pain don't tell good stories.

Tell a better one.

God of all stories, help me trust that there's a different story than the one that's easy to tell. Help me believe that pain will not be the hero.

Amen.

The mind governed by the flesh is death, but the mind governed by the Spirit is life and peace.

ROMANS 8:6, NIV

Write Your Own Confession

1. What pain are you feeling?

2. What stories are you believing about the pain?

3. Even if you can't imagine other stories yet, how could you confess your need for God's story?

NOT GOOD AT THIS

I never said I was good at this.

I never said I was good at reimagining church budgets while writing sermons and taking criticism and praying with someone close to suicide. Give me a few years, and I might get good at one of those.

Where is the place I can go to learn how to be good at this?

Where my failures won't harm anyone?

Where my missteps don't have the power to affect a whole congregation?

Where I won't have to practice with an audience?

When people tell me I've got it wrong, it's painful not because I disagree but because I've known it all along.

I never said I was good at this.

God,

Remind me of Jesus' humanity.

Remind me that he refused to be ashamed of it.

Teach me capacity for learning on the job,

for failing publicly,

for thinking of others when in the moment I just want to protect myself from embarrassment.

Provide people to do the things I'm not good at.

And in the meantime, give me uncanny, supernatural skill to do it,

if not well, at least in a way that others might see how much I need you.

May I be good at showing how to need you, wretched though it may feel to be incomplete.

Amen.

"I am exceedingly afraid and do not dare to recount Your mysteries. O good and kind Father, teach me what to say according to Your will! O reverend Father, sweet and full of grace, do not forsake me, but keep me in Your mercy!

"And again I heard the same One saying to me, 'Now speak, as you have been taught! Though you are ashes, I will that you speak.'"[3]

HILDEGARD OF BINGEN

Write Your Own Confession

1. How are you feeling not good at this calling? How do you feel you have to practice in public?

2. Confess the ways that exposure makes you hide from God.

3. Is there a way God is inviting you to need him in the discomfort and risk?

4. Give voice to a confession of trust in that invitation.

IMMEASURABLE OR IMAGINARY?

This morning I bumped into my neighbor on my daily walk. We chatted for a minute, caught up on her travels. I remembered the name of one of her dogs. After we said, "Have a nice day" and I made my way across the road, I wondered, *Should I have asked about her husband?* I'd heard he'd lost a friend last week. Is that what a pastor would have done? When am I just a neighbor, and when am I a pastor? I felt a pang of something unnameable—guilt or regret or failure.

I know I'm supposed to "make the most of every opportunity" (Ephesians 5:16). But it was early. I was barely awake, not yet in pastor mode. I was hardly even in person mode. I was just breathing and walking, trying not to obsess about things that make me anxious, trying to just avoid the mossy patch of sidewalk and be available to the sky. For the rest of the walk, I tried to make amends by smiling at every person who passed. I added a "Good morning" to the ones who met my eye.

Is it enough to just live my life as faithfully as possible and hope that somehow that makes a difference? It doesn't feel like enough. It doesn't feel like enough because I'm not consistently faithful. And even if I were, what difference would it really make in this whole neighborhood?

I tell the Lord, *To say little yeses every day is what I feel called to do. And it's what I try to do. But it never feels like enough. Is it really possible that you're working in ways I can't see? Are there things you're doing in me and in those around me that may never be named? Encourage me with whatever I need to keep investing all of my life in things I can't see.*

And then I remembered a story from yesterday. A new woman at church had shared what had first drawn her there—I'd been asked at the last minute to tell a story from the Bible at a local school. I felt dumb—I'm not trained in childhood education.

The lesson was Mary and Martha, so I put myself in Martha's place and told the story in first person. It was easy to relate to the frustration—"I'm working hard here for you, Lord; why don't I get any credit? I'd love to just sit around like Mary, but there's so much to do!" I surprised myself with the intensity of my own words, and I think most of the kids tracked with me. But when it was over I was just glad it was over, glad to be past the awkwardness of doing something I'm not good at. I walked away, leaving behind me my guilt at being underprepared and my hope that someone might remember the story.

Yesterday a new woman at church told me she'd volunteered at the school that day and she'd been moved by my story. She related to Martha and to the way I'd brought her to life. She quoted the words I'd found to express Martha's frustration, words I had no memory of saying. It was how she knew she was supposed to come to our church. All I remember of that day was feeling awkward, inadequate. How can I begin to name that as normal? How can I live in awkwardness, underpreparedness, and inadequacy as a mode of the seed-planting life?

> *Lord,*
>
> *I confess that it's hard for me to imagine that anything I do makes much of a difference.*
>
> *The meetings, the emails, the Bible study, the sermons—are they having a cumulative effect that I can't see?*
>
> *May every yes I say to you be a seed.*
>
> *Yes, I will smile at this woman who jogs by me every morning.*
>
> *Yes, I will preach these words I don't yet understand.*
>
> *Yes, I will make the most of every opportunity.*
>
> *And I will trust that those little seeds are just my part.*
>
> *Give me perseverance to keep planting seeds.*
>
> *Amen.*

"It's amazing what God can do with nothing."[4]

MOTHER TERESA

Write Your Own Confession

1. How do your daily yeses stretch you to the breaking point?

2. How does your desire to serve God tempt you away from him?

3. Write a confession of the ways you'd rather have resolution and outcomes.

4. What strength is God shaping in you even as you feel stretched? How can you confess your desire to believe how he uses the seeds you plant?

PUT IN MY PLACE

A slap in the face. At least that's how it feels. In a way I'd prefer an actual slap in the face because then the hurt would be apparent. The red welt would mark the offense. But instead I have a pounding heart, a racing mind, and yet another knot in my stomach. The conversation had been going so well. The room was engaged, offering ideas; there was momentum, and I felt hope in it. I felt God in it.

And then it happened. One person in the back raised his voice and put me in my place. He didn't like the direction of this conversation, the way I'd chosen to share my ideas. Instead of raising the concern in the spirit of the meeting, he said it with accusation, and all the positive momentum screeched to a halt. Everyone felt the lurch. But the words were directed at me, questioning my motives, my leadership. And in the moment of feeling put in my place I still had to lead, had to consider the many dynamics at work in the room.

There were newcomers among us. What would they think? Would they ever return?

There were new Christians in the room. Would it shake their faith to see Christians treating one another like this? There were some in the room whose heart now pounded like mine but with protective instincts toward me. Would I misuse their empathy or calm their concerns?

With nanoseconds to choose my response, my mind thrashed around for a way to preserve the conversation and the interests of this ministry without being led primarily by self-preservation. Because I was not feeling preserved.

Humans have good memories. And they store those memories in muscles, not only in brain cells. My heart remembered pounding like this; my stomach remembered knots like this. My eyes remembered faces like this turned in sourness. "You have no right to be here."

"Your voice is unimportant."

"Your brand of leadership is unwelcome."

"You are un-Christlike, unprofessional."

I had heard these words before, and I was hearing them again, even if no one was speaking them aloud. A little chorus with three faces from college, four faces from previous meetings sang their old songs. The urge to cry rose in my body with such force it felt more like the urge to vomit.

I had a split second—would I save face? Would I defend myself? Would I correct this naysayer? Would I apologize? Would I rethink the plan for the meeting? Or hand over the meeting for someone else to lead?

> *God,*
>> *Who do you say I am?*
>> *Do I have to be perfect to be good?*
>> *Do I have to get every word right to lead here?*
>> *Give me the words to say in this moment.*
>> *Heal me from the slaps in the face, the ones I experience*
> *today and all those I've felt in the past.*
>> *Heal those who feel the need to deal them.*
>> *Amen.*

"Leadership through self-differentiation is not easy; learning techniques and imbibing data are far easier. Nor is striving or achieving success as a leader without pain: there is the pain of isolation, the pain of loneliness, the pain of personal attacks, the pain of losing friends. That's what leadership is all about."[5]

EDWIN FRIEDMAN

Write Your Own Confession

1. How have you been slapped in the face? What is your gut reaction to slaps in the face?

2. What truth can be revealed both in the ugliness of the slap and in the ugliness of all the ways we want to react?

3. How can a slap in the face be one more opportunity to rely on the Lord? Tell it all to him.

CHAPTER SIX

I WANT TO BE FREE

O God, . . . whose service is perfect freedom . . .

THE BOOK OF COMMON PRAYER

Esther knew oppression.

As a young woman who had been orphaned and exiled, she was no stranger to subjugation.

But there's a strange freedom in having no power. When our actions make no difference, neither do our missteps. In all the other anxieties that come with powerlessness, we don't lose sleep over how many people might be affected by our decisions.

Perhaps Esther had hoped to marry and have children. Perhaps she'd imagined she'd spend her life discovering the strange freedom to be found in the constraints of family responsibility. Maybe she had looked forward to the surprising joy of the daily choice to leave a warm bed, rising early to a cold dawn because someone needs to be fed.

She had not been raised to be wife to a king. She had not been prepared to have her body, her words, or her actions thoroughly scrutinized. Now she found herself in a palace still ringing with the stories of her predecessor: "Don't be like Vashti; don't displease your king." To be invited to live in the palace, lavished daily with beauty treatments and delicacies, may, for an oppressed woman, have felt at first like freedom. Until she discovered what was expected of her, what freedoms were stripped from her.

But there was an even weightier burden yet to come, presented to Esther by her cousin, Mordecai. An edict had gone out, ordering the total annihilation of the Jews—the brutal slaughter of every man, every woman, every child. Across the empire, the news of coming destruction had set off a great mourning among the Jewish people: weeping and wailing, sackcloth and ashes. Esther, unable to bear Mordecai's despair, sent him fine, soft clothing, begging him to put aside his sackcloth, but he refused to find comfort. Instead, he let the scratching against his skin take shape in words of irritation: "Esther, you have a job to do. Go to the king. Beg for mercy for your people" (Esther 4:8, author's paraphrase).

I think Esther must have wanted to say, "You think it's fun to live in the palace, Mordecai? You think I have influence here? I'm a glorified pet! Whatever luxuries I receive are only so I can provide a service for the king's pleasure. I am a creature with no needs or opinions. Didn't you hear what happened to the last woman who spoke her mind to the king? Didn't you hear about the edicts sent across the empire demanding that women defer to their husbands? Don't you know that to even approach my husband is to dance with death?"

At this point Esther thought the choice was this: her own life or her own death. But Mordecai made it clear—the choice was this: to risk death to save her people or to certainly die along with her people. I'm sure she wanted to run away, screaming, "This is too much responsibility! I just want to be a person. I didn't ask to carry this burden. This costs too much. Just let me be. Let me live my ordinary little life."

Esther begged to be released from the weight of responsibility. Mordecai only added to the weight. But in that crisis, Mordecai spoke words that would outlive him. Mordecai made it about time. Without mentioning God's name (perhaps as a reminder of the oppression of their people's ability to worship), Mordecai drew Esther back from her angst and into a wide-open space: *There is Someone who has always been at work among our people. He has*

been there in every *"such a time as this"* moment (Esther 4:14). *He has always invited ordinary people to let their personal freedom die for the sake of the greater story. And in that personal death, freedom is possible for all.*

The choice is this: own the moment to save the life of a whole nation (and possibly die in the process) or deny the moment and lose everything. Esther had been constrained in many ways in her lifetime, and now she was constrained by others' needs. I'm sure she longed for the freedom of powerlessness. I do too. It's why we need her story.

CLAUSTROPHOBIC

It's raining. Still. Again. Usually I love the rain, and I did two weeks ago. But now I'm over it, lying here in this bed, hearing the skies open once again. I don't know what time it is, but it's dark and I'm pretty sure I should be sleeping. If I look at the time, it will make my anxiety worse. Each watery thread stretched from the clouds to the earth is one more bar keeping me indoors.

Why is it that these memories want to be unpacked when I want to sleep? Why do ordinary concerns of the day loom so large in the middle of the night? I ask God often, and the silence makes me guess that instead of answering, he wants this dark, quiet space to be filled with my prayers.

I have things to do today, things that take a peculiar kind of attention—the kind of attention that has one eye on earth and one on heaven, attending to practical matters while always remembering "things above" (Colossians 3:2, NIV). It stretches my heart, my body, and my soul, so I take care to get all those parts of me to bed on time. I can't remember the last time I finished the episode of the show we're watching, when my husband, Jamie, hasn't had to shuffle me off to bed at eight o'clock. An eight o'clock bedtime would mean a great night of sleep if I could also stay asleep through the night instead of this strange three-o'clock-in-the-morning waking to a cycle of gnawing worries.

A memory of that relationship that is still unresolved. More times than I can count, I've turned it over in my mind in the dark of sleepless nights, and I cannot comprehend what happened. A distaste over something that was said. Do I need to respond to it? A disconnection where there should be harmony. How many tears can I cry? I can't hold all this *and* carry the things the morning will ask of me.

Normally it helps to walk, to stomp around the neighborhood a bit, huffing and swinging my arms. It shakes my thoughts from their deep ruts, and the birds are always sure to give me something different to consider, calling me outside my own small head. But today the rain is keeping me in. Even walking in my raincoat means a bowed head, squinting eyes, and an inward focus.

> *Lord,*
>> *What am I to do with these things that make my heart race when it should be at rest?*
>> *You know what my day holds, all the ways I need to be present and available.*
>> *I know what I need to do this work. Let me trust that you know better.*
>> *Carry these fears; relieve me from the circling dread.*
>> *May every pore in me be a place to release what you're not asking me to carry and a place of drawing in what you have for me.*
>> *Give me courage to be porous.*
>> *Amen.*

"nighthawk"

"*n.* a recurring thought that only seems to strike you late at night—an overdue task, a nagging guilt, a looming future—which you sometimes manage to forget for weeks, only to feel it land on your shoulder once again, quietly building a nest."[1]

JOHN KOENIG

Write Your Own Confession

1. What keeps you awake at night?

2. Even if you can't force yourself to stop thinking about it, how can you list it all before the Lord, confessing your anxieties?

3. How can you confess your need for God in the sleeplessness and the fear?

TOO CLOSE FOR COMFORT

I'm feeling uncomfortable. Troubled, maybe. Humbled a bit. Conflicted.

I've just come from a gathering of about twelve people. Since they didn't know one another very well but have church in common, I asked them to share in one sentence what brought them to this congregation. As we took turns around the circle, I began to see that what I'd planned as a quick introductory exercise would become the purpose of the gathering. The "in one sentence" part of my instructions was soon forgotten as people shared how God had drawn them to this place. They told before-and-after tales: *Before, I felt anxious; now, I'm feeling more peace. Before, I felt alone; now, I'm feeling seen.*

The thing that's leaving me uncomfortable is how many of them mentioned me in their description of why they came to this church. One said I'd done their father's funeral, and it made them want to try the church. But three of the twelve mentioned my voice—it's easy to understand, it's calming in prayer, or it helps them pay attention. One said they were drawn to me for some reason after seeing my photo on the church website. Each time I was personally mentioned, I felt a bit uncomfortable, but I smiled and mumbled something like "It's all God." I'm tempted to pray: *Make me invisible so you can be visible.*

I don't want to draw people to myself. I want to draw them to God. But God seems to trust us to reveal him in all our specificity, with all our quirks and foibles. The possibility that God wants to reveal himself through me tempts me to be bland and neutral—as if I ever could! But I can never become a blank canvas that reveals nothing but pure God. And neither is that what God asks. I'm learning that he wants to reveal himself through my Mandy-ness. Which might require me to learn from him who I even am.

God,

> *I know I should try not to bring attention to myself.*
> *I know your way is the way of selflessness, of emptying.*
> *But show me when I want to empty of the wrong things.*
> *Teach me to empty of ego but not of my true nature.*
> *Teach me to set aside vanity but not personality.*
> *You came in a particular human form.*
> *A form that had a particular laugh, a particular face.*
> *You were willing to let all the glory be revealed in one particular way through that one life.*
> *Show me how I keep myself to myself.*
> *Show me how to let you be seen in this particular laugh, this particular face.*
> *I want all creation to reveal you, including this unique but ordinary little piece of creation—me.*
> *As others find the ways you're like me, may they find the ways you're like them.*
> *Amen.*

"Every one of us is shadowed by an illusory person: a false self.

"This is the man that I want myself to be but who cannot exist, because God does not know anything about him. And to be unknown of God is altogether too much privacy."[2]

THOMAS MERTON

Write Your Own Confession

1. How does it feel too close for comfort when God wants to reveal himself through you?

2. What kind of confession might express your desire to thwart that very personal revelation?

3. It seems humble, but is part of this desire evasive? Proud?

4. What do you need to confess to be able to let God use all of you as he chooses, even the parts you'd rather keep to yourself?

DYING THE WRONG DEATHS

He told us it would feel like taking up a cross. So we learn the skill of adapting to hard things. As Christians and as Christian leaders, we get used to the fact that life won't be easy, that pursuing the Kingdom might cost us everything. We trust that as we live this life like Jesus, it makes us more and more into his likeness. We carry around the death of Jesus in our bodies so the life of Jesus may be seen in our bodies (2 Corinthians 4:10).

So when our hearts are breaking, we say, *Jesus' heart broke. I'm being made like Jesus.*

And when people betray us, we say, *People betrayed Jesus. I'm being made like Jesus.*

And when the work requires more than we expected, we say, *Jesus committed to the challenges of the call. I'm being made like Jesus.*

This work is not sustainable. It wears people down. It took Jesus to the cross. It led Paul into beatings and betrayals and prison. Throughout the history of the church, it has taken missionaries far from home and martyrs to their graves. And at the same time, sometimes dying to self means speaking out when we'd rather defer.

We can get so accustomed to calming ourselves when we'd rather run away that we stop paying attention to the places where we're supposed to scream, "Something's not right here, people! It doesn't have to be this way!"

A canary in a coal mine can say, "Peace, peace" when there is no peace (see Jeremiah 6:14), as poisonous gas quietly does its deathly work. Or, instead, at the first whiff of a problem, that canary can sing its little lungs out. For its own sake and for the sake of everyone.

Some of us have been socialized to adapt. To shoulder burdens, to make room for the needs of others. In many ways, it's a Christlike posture. But one of the reasons Christ went to the cross was because he flipped tables. He spoke against the toxic gases filling the mine, killing the people. He saw what was lulling them into false peace, and he raised his head and sang his song.

Maybe the things that are slowly killing me are inherent in a life of serving others. But maybe some of the things that are slowly killing me are slowly killing all of us, our mission, and our joy.

Father, I need your help to know the difference.

Where are you calling me to adapt to what's hard?

And where is discomfort a signal for me to push back and protect us all?

Let me be resigned to every death you've called me to die.

Show me the places you've called me to cry out warning.

When I'm in a place to sense the problem before others, it's easy for me to think it's just my problem, something I should shoulder alone and not bother anyone else with.

Show me when I have a chance to say, "Something's not working here! It doesn't have to be this way!"

May those moments of unveiling be moments of freedom for us all.

Amen.

"Questions are powerful interventions. . . . They invite more light in; they subvert individual mindsets or groupthink. They challenge. If we choose to be 'comforters,' 'appeasers,' or 'know-it-all advisors,' we are not on the side of health."[3]

PETER STEINKE

Write Your Own Confession

1. How are you dying the wrong deaths? How is God calling you to adapt? How is God calling you to challenge?

2. How is the discomfort of adapting and challenging leading you to disconnect from God?

3. How might the discomfort be an opportunity to confess your dependence on him once more?

HEAVYHEARTED

I've been depressed before. That's not what this is.

I've taken on worries that are not mine to bear before. That's not what this is.

I know what it's not, but I'm not sure what it is.

It's a heaviness, that's for sure. A welling up of tears. But they're not my tears (alone).

The news this morning was one story after another of violence—a man who had torched his family, a gunman who had emptied his weapon into a train full of passengers, a despot leading war across Ukraine.

Lord, have mercy.

And then my first meeting today was with a woman traumatized by abuse, the words of abusers still ringing in her ears many years later. The scenes she described are now marked in my imagination. Some of them she's never told a soul, and she seems lighter knowing that now two hearts bear the stories.

Lord, have mercy.

And now at home there's a conversation that must be had, one that can't be done well without dredging up painful memories.

Lord, have mercy.

I hadn't planned for this day to weigh down my heart. The places I've walked this morning leave my shoes caked with mud this afternoon. They're heavy, and it's hard to take each step. I had planned to answer emails, but I just don't have it in me. I'm drawn into the empty church and remember there are some chairs that need rearranging.

My arms are glad for the work. My mind is glad for the rest. I feel something welling up in me that wants to be released. But first my rational self wants answers: *Tears again? Are they helpful tears? Shall I let them come? Will releasing these tears take us into weeks of darkness? Or is releasing them a way to release the darkness?*

I know it's the latter, so I let the tears come. My heart is being reordered with the chairs. Tears are confusing. I've learned to trust that they mean something significant is happening. But what that significance is I often don't know. They usually come with their own anxiety—is this just a normal release, or is there something going on in me that's going to take weeks to work out? Am I opening a can of very wet worms? *I have things to do! I don't have time for that!* But I need the release, so may these be the kind of tears that bring release.

Today they are that kind of tears. They're slow tears, not the kind that come with sobbing but a kind of overflowing from over-fullness. And as they release, I'm strangely calmed.

> I do not occupy myself with things
> > too great and too marvelous for me.
> But I have calmed and quieted my soul,
> > like a weaned child with its mother;
> > my soul is like the weaned child that is with me.
>
> PSALM 131:1-2, NRSV

God has invited me to know a tiny glimpse of his grief for the world. Today I've only learned about three news headlines, one woman's story, one family's pain. I don't know the millions of other violences, abuses, pains. But God has let me know he feels it and grieves it. In case I'm tempted to be overwhelmed by it, to bear things that are not mine to bear, he reminds me it's not my pain alone. And invites me to let it be carried in him. Which leaves me strangely lighter. The pain has not been taken, but the weight is carried in a heart not my own. And as I'm invited to rest in that heart, which knows but is not overcome by the pain, I sense a capacity beyond the pain. I sense a grave that knows life, an emptiness that knows abundance. Curled up in this dark cave, I can hear the trickling of water all around me, bringing life to all it touches, a tiny giggle that promises great joy to come.

My God,

Let me know the difference between my pain and yours.
Let me know the sameness between my pain and yours.
Let me bear not too much, not too little.
Let me know what to do with the weight.
Let me remember to bring back to you what is yours,
to rest in you like a weaned child,
to listen for the ripple of joy in the darkness.
As I know your grief, give me also a glimpse of your joy,
which is greater than every heartbreak.
Give me courage to enter the darkness with others
and faith to imagine how life might begin there.
For all of us.
Amen.

"I misconstrued ministry as full-time security in the womb of the church. . . . The call to pastoral ministry is a call out of the womb of the church into the perilous and painful role of being pregnant with the church, of giving birth to it, of nursing it and raising it."[4]

DAVID HANSEN

Write Your Own Confession

1. What weighs down your heart? How does it draw you into darkness?

2. What words might begin to confess the ways you avoid hard things? The ways you carry things you're not being asked to carry?

3. What words might begin to confess your need for God's help in knowing what he asks of you in dark places?

HOUNDED

It began as whispers so I wouldn't notice the crescendo. But now the voices are nagging, incessant. I've become accustomed to them, so it's taken me some time to even stop to name them. Maybe I've been afraid to do so because it means confronting the possibility that I'm losing my sanity. When there are accusations in your head all day long, is that a sign that something's seriously wrong with you? Or is it just tiredness? Hormones? Spiritual forces? Some other thing? It's only now, as I confront these questions, that I'm able to release the tension in my shoulders and take a breath. It's only now that I'm conscious of how exhausting it is to tune out voices clamoring in my ears all day long, how much energy it takes to override their lies, how much I've been missing the silence that's usually mine to fill with daydreams and prayer and nothing at all.

I don't know what these *hormones or spiritual forces or some other thing* is. But I know it's been torment. I know I've hunched my shoulders like someone's been yelling in my ear all day. I know it's taken all my energy to be present to others. I know that if anyone has said anything that's reminded me even vaguely of the voices, it's been more than I could bear.

- *How can God use you if you don't even have a plan yet?*
- *What's the point of all this work?*
- *Why do you even care about this place?*
- *You're wearing yourself out, and for what? Where is God? Why isn't he providing?*
- *You're investing everything in this ordinary place. Why bother?*
- *If God is good and God called you here, what are you doing wrong to make the work so hard?*
- *You're supposed to feel peace and joy. Why are you always tired and overwhelmed?*

- *If you were mature, you'd have your life in better balance by now. What are you doing wrong that you aren't on top of things yet?*
- *Other people in your kind of work know how to juggle all the challenges without breaking down.*

It's hard to even try to capture these. They don't all present themselves in words but in unnamed fears and unspoken shames, all of which carve away at me a little at a time. Even as I type them, I feel a tiny twitch in my left cheek, a remnant of my week of squinting to keep all this out of my head and heart.

Father, I work really hard here. And yet it still feels like it's never enough.

And I take off every Monday for Sabbath. And I get to bed on time most nights. And yet it still feels like it's never enough.

I walk in nature every morning. I listen to an audio Bible and journal and pray. And yet it still feels like it's never enough.

I'm still overwhelmed, still tired, still left feeling unprepared.

I sense you inviting me to be like the small boy holding up his little lunch.

My hands shake with the offering. I see the morsels; I see the multitude.

I'm tempted to keep my offering in my pocket. Too small, too ordinary.

I'm invited to get used to the smallness.

As I pray, I hear the butcher-birds in duet. I tune my ear to pick out each bird's part, smiling to know how each bird trusts that her few, small notes will join with the few, small notes of the other. Each gives full voice to her part, trusting

that other notes will fill the spaces between her own so that
a complete tune will fall on the ears of a weary walker.

Let me offer up my sandwich, miserable though it seems.
Let me sing my song, even though I only know a few notes.
Make it a feast; make it a chorus.
I can't wait.
Amen.

"Lord, look upon my weakness and wretchedness, for both are indeed well known to You. Have pity on me and *pull me out of this mire before I become imbedded in it* and totally dejected. . . .

"Though I do not altogether consent to these temptations, never-theless, their pursuit after me is most annoying and so distressing that I grow weary living under such constant tension. . . .

"Strengthen me with courage from heaven."[5]

THOMAS À KEMPIS

Write Your Own Confession

1. How are you tired, overwhelmed, tempted to despair?

2. Confess however it tempts you to avoid, to shrink.

3. What is God inviting you to believe? How might you confess your desire to believe it, even if it seems ridiculous?

JOYFUL

I feel good today. Happy, even. I may even go as far as to say joyful.

It takes a surprising amount of faith to embrace that, to lead from that.

I make the choice every day to have hope, to imagine a possibility that there is more to life and ministry than there seems, to live as if it's real so it has a chance to become real.

But sometimes it's not a choice; it's just natural. In this trying season, those days of natural joy are few and far between. So I doubt them.

I doubt this is real.

I doubt I can trust it.

I doubt it will last.

So today I find myself analyzing it—there's a physical feeling in my stomach, something bubbling up. And there's a feeling in my mind—a clarity, a creative energy, a looking up from my striving. There's something in my spirit—a relief that this doesn't have to always be hard.

But it has been hard for a long time. Family life has been hard, work life has been hard, church relationships, navigating change and grief and mental- and physical-health issues, all hard. Some of these things have changed. Some haven't changed; I'm just feeling less overwhelmed by them today.

(Maybe it's just that this week someone else is preaching.)

Why do I trust negative feelings but force positive feelings to justify themselves? Negative feelings, by their nature, never promise anything, so they can never disappoint. It takes me time to test the positivity—can it take my weight? What if it collapses under me? It's a conscious effort to choose to trust it's worth the risk. I know I'll be sad and overwhelmed and anxious again—more reason to receive whatever this is!

The more I think about this joy, the more it makes sense. I've been working for nine months to break up hard ground here. I've cleared stones and weeds from the garden, and I'm seeing tiny shoots that finally have the light and space to break through the ground.

I do believe that the Spirit has a way about him. He just wants to grow, to bear fruit, to flourish. Wherever he's given space—in one human life, in a community, in the world—he can't help but bring life. Much of our work is hard because in addition to sowing those seeds, we're also cutting back everything that doesn't look like life. That cutting back takes discernment, brings conflict, and is just plain hard work, demanding everything of our bodies, minds, and spirits, requiring us to bring all our gifts and stretch all our places of nongifts.

God of all joy,
    I believe that even as you see the brokenness, violence, and despair of this world, there is something bubbling up in you, greater than all the pain.
    May I learn your capacity to hold joy.
    Help me get over my fear of being disappointed, of looking naïve.
    And when I no longer feel the joy, give me courage to live it anyway.
    Amen.

"Optimism and hope are radically different attitudes. Optimism is the expectation that things—the weather, human relationships, the economy, the political situation, and so on—will get better. Hope is the trust that God will fulfill God's promises to us in a way that leads us to true freedom. The optimist speaks about concrete changes in the future. The person of hope lives in the moment with the knowledge and trust that all of life is in good hands."[6]

HENRI NOUWEN

Write Your Own Confession

1. Is it hard to embrace joy? What do you fear might happen if you do?

2. How are you tempted to look cool, avoid disappointment?

3. How is God calling you into his joy and asking you to trust him with the possibility that the joy may be fleeting?

4. Shape a confession of whatever you need to release.

CONFORMED

The day began at 4:30 a.m. again. Not by my choice but by the choice of whatever jostles a heart awake. Maybe it's not so much a heart but a bladder that wakes first. So as I shuffled to the bathroom, I asked the question that often comes first: *What's today?*

And before the name *Tuesday* was formed in my mind, I knew what day it was from the dread that surfaced. Tuesday is the first day of my workweek. Monday is a day to just be Mandy the person, Mandy the child of God. It takes me walking, it sends me napping, sometimes reading, drawing, crying, dancing. Just being.

But Tuesday asks me to conform to the needs of this place. The gifts required by this community are the gifts I will bring. The gifts that are not currently needed here I will set aside. And the skills this community needs me to have I will learn, even if they stretch me to breaking. The questions this place asks, the problems it has, will become my questions, my problems. The people here are the people I will serve and love (whether I like them or not). The needs they have will decide how I pray and teach and lead. It's a conformity I chose when I was commissioned to this work:

> "Mandy, do you confess Jesus Christ as Lord?"
> "I do."
> "Do you believe . . . ?"
> "I do."
> "Do you receive . . . ?"
> "I do."
> "Do you embrace . . . ?"
> "I do."

"Will you submit . . . ?"

"I will."

"Will you take part in the work? Will you share in the life and witness?"

"I will. I will."

"Will you endeavor . . . ?"

"Yes. Yes. Yes."

All that submission, endeavoring, and undertaking I chose. It's necessary for the kind of commitment required. It's what keeps me from pretending I didn't see the church roof leaking, even though it's my day off. But at 4:30 a.m., still drowsy with the indulgence of sleep, I smart at the invitation to conform again. The expansiveness of dreaming does not want to be squeezed into the limitations of one place.

The quietness of the bathroom allows a moment of waking—this is temptation. The freedom I think I want is a freedom to be unshaped, unused.

The Lord disciplines those he loves (Hebrews 12:6). He confines to bring expansion.

"We are the agents of the Creative Spirit in this world. Real advance in the spiritual life, then, means accepting this vocation with all it involves."[7]

EVELYN UNDERHILL

Lord,

I believe in a God who brings freedom.
I've known that God, that freedom.
This doesn't feel like freedom.
You don't seem like that God.
I'm familiar with the stories of the martyrs,
the dramatic ways they gave their lives in the name of following Jesus.
Is there also a slow kind of martyrdom in giving a life over decades?
Is this what Paul meant by "poured out like a drink offering"[8]*?*
Is this what he meant by "present your bodies as a living sacrifice"[9]*?*
Slow sacrifices of being stretched thin by the needs of others, overwhelmed by meetings,
death by a thousand paper cuts.
Give me courage to live whatever life you call me to live
and to die whatever death you call me to die, ordinary and drawn out though it may be.
Reveal your resurrection even in the slow kinds of death.
Amen.

Write Your Own Confession

1. How do you feel crushed by conformity to the needs of your community?

2. How do you long for freedom to just do what you want?

3. Are there ways you are longing for independence from God?

4. Confess your desire for freedom from his shaping.

5. Confess how you choose to let him expand you in all the places you feel confined.

CHAPTER SEVEN

I WANT TO FEEL STRONG

In me there is darkness,
But with you there is light;
I am lonely, but you do not leave me;
I am feeble in heart, but with you there is help;
I am restless, but with you there is peace.
In me there is bitterness, but with you there is patience;
I do not understand your ways,
But you know the way for me.

DIETRICH BONHOEFFER, PRAYER WRITTEN CHRISTMAS 1943

A prophet?!

Prophets know the mind of God. And prophets have eloquent words and are always ready to speak on God's behalf. They know when to speak fire and when to speak comfort. And they know when to not speak at all. They're poets adept in the medium of silence and sound, performance artists playing out odd metaphors for the instruction of all the people.

God, what makes you think I could be a prophet?!

And prophet to the nations?!

Prophets command attention. Prophets fill space with their bodies, their words. They have no concern for rules of behavior, little regard for kings. Prophets to nations have much to say, and they say it to many. Prophets have much to lose.

Maybe if I were older, Lord?

We all like the idea of hearing God's voice. Until we remember how often his voice asks impossible things. Jeremiah wasn't asking to be a prophet. What made God think Jeremiah was the one to appoint over nations and kingdoms, to uproot and tear down, to destroy and overthrow, to build and to plant (Jeremiah 1:10)? When this call comes to Jeremiah's small ears, his heart aches with its own faint pulse. His tongue withers. With desperation he scans every corner of his own self to find some sign of strength—feet planted firmly or a chest puffed out or a voice that might fill the halls of kings. And he finds what he expected to find: nothing.

When a man is given a task, it only makes sense to assess his own capacity. If someone had come to Jeremiah's door asking for a forest to be felled, he would have pointed them in the direction of the woodsman; if a tapestry to be woven, toward the hands of the weavers flying at their looms. He doesn't have the skill or the tools to be any kind of prophet, much less a prophet to the nations. He is too young; he cannot speak. *Move along, God. Find someone else.*

God smirks at Jeremiah's shallow knowledge of his own self. God agrees that Jeremiah is too young, unskilled, inarticulate. What God knows about Jeremiah is that God knows Jeremiah, that God knew Jeremiah long before Jeremiah knew himself. God knows the call is not dependent on age because Jeremiah's call existed before Jeremiah did. God knows this call cannot be about being articulate, because when Jeremiah was set apart, he did not even have a mouth yet (Jeremiah 1:5). God knows the power of his own call, his own words, his own sending, and his own ability to make a young man into a fortified city to stand against a whole land.

When Jeremiah has finished scrounging inside himself for some sign of competence, he's finally empty enough to hear where to look for competence: *God will send you, God will command you, God has put the words in your mouth, God has appointed you, God is with you, and God will rescue you. You have no words, but*

God has put words in your mouth. You are inconsequential, but God has made you a bronze wall. You are porous, but God has made you impenetrable.

The only competence required of Jeremiah is his obedience.

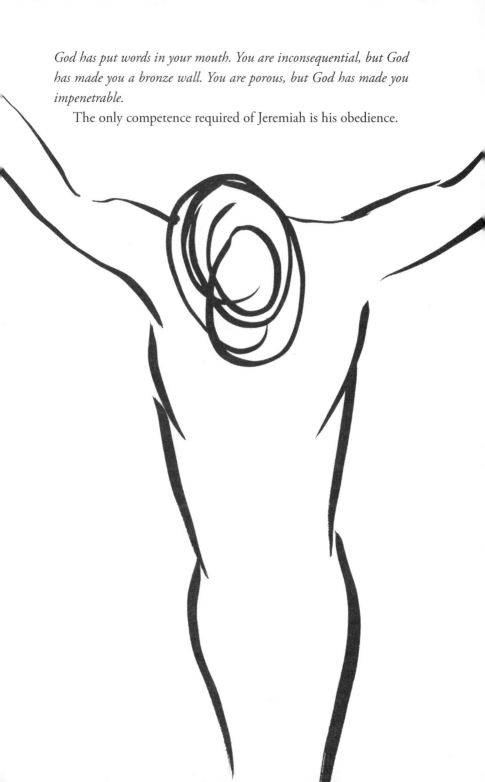

RIDICULOUS

I've read the Triumphal Entry story a thousand times. It's never struck me as funny before. Joyous, yes. Expectant, yes. But never funny. The humor begins with Zechariah 9, proclaiming a great promise of the coming King, triumphant and victorious. We know that image—warrior on a warhorse, ruler on a steed, emblazoned with glorious armor, flowing robes. Then, in the same breath, Zechariah adds "humble and riding on a donkey" to that image (verse 9, NRSV). And not just a donkey but the foal of a donkey!

Jesus knows what he's doing as he plays out this dramatic scene with enough kingly things in place to make the crowd sing, "Blessed is the king who comes in the name of the Lord!" (Luke 19:38, NRSV). Their minds turn to triumphant King David. Did they also remember David the littlest, the last to be chosen? David with his sling and pebbles? David, dancing with abandon?

I think Jesus did. And so, at this moment, when they're looking at him in that particular way, expectations high, Jesus redirects their attention. He's willing to be a bit ridiculous. Not to make light of the moment. Oh no, this moment and those that come after it have great gravity. The gravity of death and the even greater gravity of life. And so, in the weight of what is unfolding, Jesus has a lightness about him, a strange irreverence, straddling this little beast, so small that Jesus' feet almost drag on the ground.

I like to imagine Jesus' smirking subversion: *You have your hopes set on a powerful, earthly ruler? I'll give you a man on a donkey.*

This scene reminds me of those stories of a seeker pursuing a great treasure. After many mishaps, they usually find themselves in a temple or on a mountaintop, finally discovering this long-sought prize, only to open the box and find inside not the treasure they expected but emptiness. Or sometimes even a mirror. The message? "You thought you wanted a treasure, but the greater gift is a moment to ask what treasure you really seek." Jesus is willing to be a bit ridiculous to disrupt our sense of the treasure we seek.

Yesterday in Bible study the woman beside me started shaking. She'd told me she has panic attacks, but I've never seen her having one before. I held her hand and asked her to breathe. I invited the group to pray for her. And gradually the shaking stopped.

The woman beside her whispered, in awe, "Mandy, how do you carry all the burdens of a congregation? I could never do that." The look in her eyes was delicious. I wanted to live there in that warm admiration. Until I remembered Jesus on his donkey.

"Oh," I replied with a shy smile. "I'm not strong. I'm ridiculous. I don't know how to fix this. All I know is that God is powerful. All I know is to ask God for help."

People will look to us for their hope, will be tempted to let the journey finish with us: "I came to church looking for God and found a pastor." When they look to us, may they see us looking to Someone Else.

Father,

I confess that I love that look of admiration in people's faces. Whatever they've turned on presidents and professors they turn on me, and it's like basking in warm sunshine.

But I don't want what comes with it: expectations of deity.

Thank you that even you, God of all creation, entered into human life in a way that refused to be shaped by our consumption of you.

Thank you that you found no shame in ordinary humanness.

Thank you that you were willing to be wonderfully, sacredly ridiculous.

Teach me to be the same.

Amen.

"Is it possible, I wonder, to say that it is only when you hear the Gospel as a wild and marvelous joke that you really hear it at all? Heard as anything else, the Gospel is the church's thing, the preacher's thing, the lecturer's thing. Heard as a joke—high and unbidden and ringing with laughter—it can only be God's thing."[1]

FREDERICK BUECHNER

Write Your Own Confession

1. How are you tempted to be admired?

2. How does it draw attention—your own and others'—away from God?

3. What do you need to confess to release that?

4. What do you need to confess to be ridiculous in the way of Jesus?

DOUBTING GOD'S HELP

Every Wednesday I feel it: the expectation that by Sunday I will have at least twenty minutes of content that's scriptural and thoughtful and articulate, meeting the needs of young and old, regardless of their attention span and personality type. But on Wednesday morning I usually have nothing. I don't feel God's power. He hasn't dropped an instant sermon in my lap. When I don't have power and answers, I've been taught what to do: work so hard it bypasses any creativity, any spirituality.

This morning I walked, as I do every morning. I wanted to hear a kookaburra. They only chortle at certain times, and I haven't yet figured out what those are, but it's a gift to be nearby when the time is finally right. Instead, this morning I was treated to a duet from two butcher-birds, a haunting song I always thought was the song of one bird until I watched two on a wire, bobbing as they took their turn in the tune. I stopped to watch, to pick out the parts in their duet. It wasn't a kookaburra, but I received it.

The thing I have to repent of most is my agenda, my unspoken expectation: *If God were powerful,* this *would be happening.* And since those things aren't happening, I can't imagine God at work. But today I'm wondering, *What if butcher-birds are whistling all around me and I'm so busy straining to hear a kookaburra that my ears are unable to enjoy what's actually happening?* My doubt doesn't always take the form of philosophical inquiry, of questioning God's existence in some theoretical way. Instead it's usually on a practical level: I look at the world around me and strain to see any sign of God at work.

Maybe Wednesday should be a day not only to look forward at sermons but also to look back at sermons. To remember that the finely honed paragraph I felt so proud of last Thursday was not the moment that most resonated last Sunday. The words that most connected, that shook me as they left my body, were words I had not expected to say. These words did not come from my busy, anxious self but from the places in me where the Spirit groans. I saw how those words landed with others, how those words disrupted others, set up something singing in them in that same place where the Spirit sings in me. How can I look forward to next Sunday with the power of *that* in my bones? How can I work this week with the promise of that power, dormant in me, waiting to be woken by the Spirit, who writes every good sermon?

Powerful God,
    Forgive me for the agendas that I set for you.
    Thank you that you won't be contained in the ways I want to contain you,
        won't be contorted to the shapes I have made for you,
        won't be controlled by the tasks I set for you.
    As much as I think I'd like it, I don't want a pet—
I need a God.
    I need a God who is beyond me: beyond my fathoming, beyond my control,
        beyond the whims of what seems important to this small heart.
    Thank you that you care about what's burdening me today and that, at the same time,
        you're not redirected in every way I'm redirected.
    Give me courage to trust that you are powerful even though you're not working in the ways, in the places, in the timing that I'd prefer.
    Help me be willing to be interrupted by how you are at work in me, around me.
    Let me not miss one way you're speaking, acting, or guiding.
    Let me know how to jump in wherever you are.
    Amen.

"All of the cultural behaviors of seeking comfort or preferences or power or certainty or leverage are constantly at play. [Scripture] provides us with another perspective—learn to see what God sees, to discern what God is doing, to receive and engage God's initiatives."[2]

MARK LAU BRANSON AND ALAN ROXBURGH

Write Your Own Confession

1. How is it hard for you to let God work through you a little at a time?

2. Confess the ways you'd rather set agendas for God.

3. Remember the times you've seen God work because you'd released your agenda.

4. Confess how you choose to release to God's ways, God's timing.

SPINNING

I was shuffling around the house in my slippers, sleepily moving toward bed when the news came. The cheery ping of the text gave no warning for what it carried. We were caught midconversation. We read the text together and were silent. For a moment at least, we were silent. And then the questions began. They poured out in our prayers as we sat at the foot of our bed. And they continued through the night, disrupting our dreams.

This morning it's cloudy, and that seems fitting for a day when I wake to the disturbing memory of late-night news. A short text that opened up so many questions. My mind swims. Every news report I listen to this morning somehow leads me back to these questions. Every moment to reflect, to pray, to prepare for my day I find myself here again, asking, *How did my mind find a way back to this turning over and over of all the unknowable things?*

In ninety minutes I meet with someone about baptism, then a Bible study group arrives at my house. And after that a lunch meeting and then a phone call with my intern. And today some emails need my attention. I need to write my pastoral newsletter and start some notes for a sermon. Oh, I could take the day off, but this Sunday a service still needs to happen. At what point is a shock so much I need to ask for someone else to lead the service? At what point is it just the way life is, the way we have to proclaim truth even with questions? Even if I took the day off, the week off, would it help? I'd only have more time to spend asking questions that can't be answered. Is there some way that pondering the mysteries of God as a preacher on behalf of a congregation is the very thing I need as I ponder this new, private conundrum? Maybe I'm hungry for God this week in a way that will make my work more meaningful? Maybe I'm hungry for God this week in a way that will make my faith more fervent? So I rest as I can, sometimes in a way that means not working and sometimes in a way that means praying *Let me rest in you* even as I work.

> *God of all mystery,*
> > *You know beyond.*
> > *You are before and after.*
> > *For every unanswerable question, there is you.*
> > *For every unknowable thing, there is you.*
> > *May we rest in the comfort that even if we have no*
> *answers, we have you.*
> > *Give me grace to lead others even as I feel myself*
> *spinning.*
> > *Amen.*

"Our ministry will always be practiced through our own conflicted selves."[3]

WALTER BRUEGGEMANN

Write Your Own Confession

1.   How do you find yourself spinning right now?

2.   What are you grasping for? Confess the ways you look for short-term fixes in the spinning.

3.   How is God asking you to reach for him? Confess your choice to once more find something solid in him, even if you still feel dizzy.

(ALLOWED TO BE) ANGRY?

All night my dreams were of floorboards rolling like waves and something like seasickness. Letters left unanswered in a forgotten mailbox and feeling lost in a place that should feel familiar. The sheets had a mind of their own and needed to be wrestled so often that finally, by 4:00 a.m., I gave up and got out of bed.

I think I'm angry. But anger is frowned upon in my family, in my faith, and for my gender. It's "unbecoming," "inappropriate," "violent" by necessity. It's just not what we do. But what else to call this feeling?

I work so hard every day to watch my words to make sure I'm shaping a welcoming community, offering a sense of unity in difference, making space for people's quirks, and giving the benefit of the doubt. I read and reread my emails to be sure I've found a way to be honest and generous. But not everyone does that work. Not everyone chooses to filter, to consider their own emotions, to protect others from their pain. Not everyone is aware of the emotional wake they leave.[4] Not everyone sees how much work they make for others when they avoid the work they need to do in themselves.

Today I'm seasick in someone else's emotional wake. Instead of the leisurely prayer walk I'd planned today, I'm dissecting my own responses. How much of my response is just my own junk, things I have to work through, stuff I need to let go? I'd rather not be spending my time on this today.

I'm starting to wonder if I'm jealous that some people get to let their anxieties leak out onto others. Do they have a deeper trust in the community than I do? Trusting that we will all just absorb it and love them anyway? Is there something wrong with me that I don't feel the confidence to go there? Is my unwillingness to share my unprocessed thoughts and feelings a sign that I underestimate the grace of others?

Maybe I'm having a hard time coming to terms with my anger

because I'm not sure there will be allowance for it. How can I find a space where my frustration will be received? Where I will be received? Is there a place where a woman, a pastor, a Christian can be unfiltered (even just for a few moments)? To just vent the ugliness so that the truth can be picked clean from what I need to let go? There is some goodness hidden in the indignation, but it's hard to find it without doing more damage along the way.

It takes all my energy to name this as anger. Anger is just not very nice. All morning I've been reading about the problem of suppressing true things, remembering the importance of honesty and integrity. ("Anger is an assertion of rights and worth. . . . It is rational thought and irrational pain. . . . In anger, whether you like it or not, there is truth. . . . It is both powerlessness and power. . . . Anger is the expression of hope.")[5] Expressing this feeling in a healthy way probably requires some stomping or yelling, but I just feel like stewing.

It's taken me until midmorning to remember I should talk to God about it. In prayer I sense something like a gentle smile and words like *That's what forgiveness is for.* I balk at the thought of a forgiveness that minimizes the injustice. How can forgiveness carry real power unless it's actually unburdening a weight of actual pain? It's a cheap forgiveness, not forgiveness at all. But I feel God asking me to count the cost and pay it anyway. To feel the sourness in my mouth. And to spit.

I'm starting to wonder something new: Maybe my anger with this person comes from my feeling that they've ruined a perfect thing *I've* made. But I know that anything good happening grows from *God's* grace being sufficient in whatever small, broken thing I offer. I've been practicing the promise that God's grace is sufficient in my own weakness, my own stupidity and immaturity. Is God asking me to trust that his grace will also have to be sufficient for the stupid, immature things that *others* do? That even if we all mess up this thing we're trying to create here, God can use it, maybe not to create the thing we thought we were making, but to do a greater thing?

> *Father, show me what indignation you're asking me to*
> *let die.*
> *And show me what truth needs to be spoken, not just*
> *for my sake but for the sake of us all.*
> *Give me courage to let go of the thing I'd love to say.*
> *And give me courage to speak the things I'd rather*
> *not say.*
> *Help me trust that there's space for me to be less guarded.*
> *Help me trust the community's capacity to give me grace.*
> *Forgive our debts as we forgive our debtors.*
> *Amen.*

"There is no shortage of spiritual directors in our life, for our spiritual directors are the people we live with. They place upon us unbearable burdens, they give us unexplainable gifts, they grind us like wheat."[6]

JAMES FINLEY

Write Your Own Confession

1. How do you feel angry? How do you feel about the possibility that you're angry?

2. Confess any desire to control your own emotions and the emotions of others.

3. What is the opportunity here to trust whatever God is offering you, even if it feels unsatisfying in the short term?

4. How can you confess belief in God as the source of what you actually need?

DESPERATE TOGETHER ❧

I've had two long conversations today, one about the church on a state level, one more local. Both headed in the same direction— not enough people, leaders, training, money, energy, or time. And too much loss, grief, and disruption. Neither conversation ended with any answers. But both ended with prayer, deep prayers of longing, with tears and allusions to the groaning of all creation (Romans 8:22).

After the first conversation, a few of us lingered to comfort one another, to say, "You're not imagining it—what you're facing is hard! I don't know the way forward, but you're not alone." And after the second conversation, there was laughter as we described how much chocolate we now needed and wondered where the closest chocolate shop might be. It was the laughter of people who've shared all their woes with one another and with God and now, on the other side of despair, find a ridiculous release. Life is crazy, and we can't control it, so we might as well eat some chocolate. We're on this roller coaster whether we like roller coasters or not. We can grasp the seat in terror. That would make sense. Or we can thrust our arms into the rushing air, opening our mouths to scream that roller-coaster scream, from the place where anxiety and excitement are almost the same.

> *Father, if you are Father over all this upheaval*
> *and have been in every upheaval through the ages,*
> *what does that mean for us?*
> *I'm wondering now if, after the space to lament and grieve,*
> *to be desperate together,*
> *there's a strangely peaceful place to console one another*
> *and if we find you in one another there.*

We're looking for a different kind of peace, one where everything around us is predictable.

Show us the peace you work in us, even the uncanny sense of abandon, even when the world is crumbling.

Amen.

"Can our very weakness be the means for God to work here in new ways? . . .

"I believe this could be a time of revival if we let weakness be the agent for God's tabernacling."[7]

MARVA DAWN

Write Your Own Confession

1. How do you feel desperate? What upheavals are you experiencing?

2. How do you just want to know everything will be okay? Where do you look for that certainty?

3. Confess belief that God can be your safe place even if the confusion remains.

WANTING IDOLS

I've often rolled my eyes at the Israelites in the wilderness, thinking, *If I'd seen the seas part and been led by the pillar of fire, I would have no need for a golden calf.* But this morning I can understand their desire for a golden calf. In wilderness times, we want visible evidence that we're getting somewhere. We want to point to a program we created, some kind of momentum building, new people coming. Something.

I know people are looking to me for guidance, for results, for answers. It's a moment to choose whether I'll make idols. It's a funny unspoken back-and-forth between the pastor and her people as they turn to her and say, "Will you be my God?" She looks within herself and sees she has nothing to offer that feels like enough to be God, and she has a moment to choose—to throw together something that will suffice or to be not enough once more. Is it our call to every day be a bit disappointing so that people are forced to look to God? Perhaps it's our call not only to be a bit disappointing but also to get over our own surprise at that so that we can even pastor people through their disappointment with us. We can be ashamed that we are not God for them. Or we can laugh and say, "Ha, oh dear. No, you're mistaken. I'm empty, but I know where to look to be filled. Will you look to him with me?"

As I left the house to preach this morning, Jamie asked how I felt about the sermon. I called behind me: "It's a bit ordinary. Once more I have an opportunity to be an object lesson of God's grace at work in weakness. In every way I'm a bit disappointing, may it invite folks to turn to him."

God,

Forgive me for the ways I want to have solid, measurable things that feel real.

Your promise of strength in weakness feels vague.

Your promise of yeast in dough feels nebulous.

Your promise of all things being made new stretches my imagination to the breaking point.

Your time line is beyond my patience.

I want things obvious; I want things now.

For me, for us all.

Help me trust in actual Reality, in and all around me.

Help me trust that spiritual things are not metaphorical just because we can't see them.

Expand my imagination for the power of your Spirit at work in me, at work in us.

Amen.

"Leave all resultings, do the next thing."[8]

OLD SAXON POEM

Write Your Own Confession

1. Which idols most tempt you?

2. How does your own desire for idols tempt you to be an idol for others?

3. What measurable things would make you feel more solid?

4. Confess any way that that desire could instead be for God's realness.

CHAPTER EIGHT

I WANT TO GIVE UP

"The spirit is willing . . ."
	MARK 14:38

Do not be deceived, Wormwood. Our cause is never more in danger than when a human, no longer desiring, but still intending, to do our Enemy's will, looks round upon a universe from which every trace of Him seems to have vanished, and asks why he has been forsaken, and still obeys.

    C. S. LEWIS, *THE SCREWTAPE LETTERS*

I wonder if he felt like bursting. He was polite and calm at the supper, but something was welling up in him, and he couldn't contain it any longer. He needed to be outside, to make space for whatever wanted to crack him open. There he could let it leak from him, heavy drops against the ground.

Sometimes we're called to do things we cannot do.

Sometimes we do them anyway.

His prayers are now recorded for us in a nice, tidy font on crisp, white pages, but I wish I could have heard the ragged anguish escaping his lips. In it I would hear my own.

His words are the opposite of what he's tempted to say:

Instead of "God, who are you to me?" he says, "Father."
Instead of "What difference can you even make?" he says,
   "You can do all things"!

When he's tempted to keep his deepest desires to himself, he
  begs, "Please just take this cup away."
And when he's tempted to hold his life close, to imagine he
  can control his own destiny, he responds with "Not my
  will but yours" (see Mark 14:36).

As much as we'd like to feel God's closeness all the time, we
can't force those feelings.

And as much as we'd like to understand God, no amount of
intellectual wrangling can stretch our minds around his mysteries.

One of the few things we can control in this world is our own
will.

And so, even when we don't feel it, even when we don't understand, even when we want to run to the farthest place from this,
we can still choose to say, "Not my will but yours."

There's nothing in the story that says the Crucifixion couldn't happen until Jesus had submitted to it, no sense that the soldiers were
waiting nearby until they heard his words of acceptance. But I do wonder if it would have gone differently without Jesus' hard work of the
will. Did "Not my will but yours" allow Jesus to heal a severed ear? Did
"Not my will but yours" keep his tongue still when his accusers were
already convinced of his guilt? Did "Not my will but yours" give Jesus
the grace to also say, "They don't know what they are doing" (Luke
23:34)? When the centurion who oversaw Jesus' death said, "Surely
this man was the Son of God!" (Mark 15:39, NIV), it was because he
saw how Jesus died. Was there something about the way Jesus died that
was different because Jesus had said, "Not my will but yours"?

Every day I feel adrenaline pooling in my feet, waiting for the
slightest permission to run from this cup.

Every day I want to cry, "Take this cup from me!"

But every day, even when I don't feel the right feelings and have
no understanding, I can choose once more to say, "Not my will
but yours." And every day I'm here again, asking God to expand

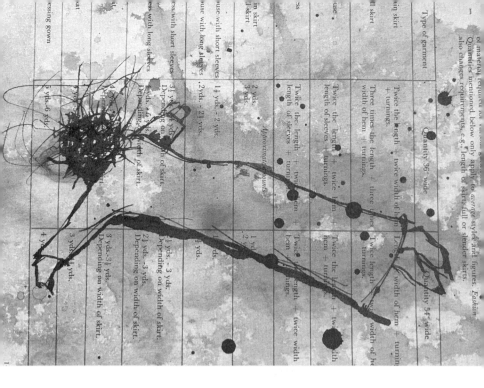

my imagination that something new is possible in a little life that has given itself.

Your will be done. Your will be done. Your will be done.

Your Kingdom come. Your Kingdom come. Your Kingdom come.

On earth as it is in heaven.

Sometimes we're called to do things we cannot do.

Sometimes we do them anyway.*

---

* **NOTE:** Stopping to take a break is not giving up. Please do not read these words as one more directive to override your need to stop, to rest, to walk away from a dangerous or unhealthy situation. Discern with your spiritual director, your counselor, or a trusted friend whether God is calling you to make a change in your situation, short-term or for good.

Stepping away to rest, to recover, and to be safe is not giving up. Giving up is choosing to act as if God were not good or powerful. Stopping to rest or move away to a healthier place can be a way to trust even more deeply in God's power and goodness, trusting that God will provide a space for us to breathe, that God will carry the burdens we thought were only ours. And sometimes, when we've discerned all that, we still decide to stay in the hard place, deciding each day to be there one more day.

READY FOR BREAKTHROUGH

I'm not good at knowing when to keep trying and when to wipe the dust off my feet.

Perseverance is necessary. But when is it foolishness?

Perseverance takes us beyond our normal self-preservation, what is reasonable and possible, what we'd choose. And once we're out there in that formless place, overriding our own reason, how do we even know *Okay, now* this *is a sign we've gone too far?*

I trust that God parts rivers. He's done it literally and metaphorically. I know that his way is to invite us to dip a toe in first, an act of trust, to show we really do intend to walk straight ahead, through what is now only water. That wet foot is an outward expression of our choice to imagine dry land when we only see a river. I've had my foot in this river a long time. Now it's both feet, now ankles, now knees. I just keep wading in, waiting, calling back to those on shore, "Any moment now! God is faithful!"

Knee-deep, hip-deep, waist-deep.

Waiting . . .

Did I mishear God?

Is this the wrong river? The wrong timing?

I know that our story is one of perseverance and mystery.

And I also trust that God is a God who does miracles, sometimes suddenly.

Maybe the breakthrough God has in store is not the breakthrough I'm longing for. I long for signs of help, of friends for the journey, of momentum building. I long for obvious signs of God's action. Not for the sake of a show, proof, but because without God's help, we have nothing. Is the breakthrough God has for me today to teach me not to expect sudden breakthrough?

A sound at my shoulder lifts my head. A butcher-bird sings at my window, just inches away, a loud, reedy song. He is here; I am here. And he sings again, and I see he has tiny feathers, like whiskers beside his beak. Rainwater beads on his back. He does not solve my problem, answer my questions, or resolve my pain. But he is here, and I am here.

Breakthrough may come in obvious, sudden ways. Waters may part.

But for now, I can do the next good thing. I know what to do today. I can do it again.

Father,

Today I asked for a particular provision.

It seems, in my way of seeing things, that nothing is possible here unless, until . . .

Sometimes my instincts are right: It's time for wiping the mud of this particular river off these feet.

Sometimes my instincts are way off: It's still time to wait.

I'm still feeling waist-deep in this river.

I still can imagine the dry land underneath.

If you tell me I have the wrong river, I'll move.

If you tell me to wade further in, I'll do it.

Give me perseverance in places where you're saying, "Not yet."

Give me wisdom in places where you're saying, "Look for a new river."

And give me breakthrough.

Sometimes you bring breakthrough.

Amen.

"Let us dare to test God's resources. . . . Let us ask Him to kindle in us and keep aflame that passion for the impossible that shall make us delight in it with Him, till the day when we shall see it transformed into a fact."[1]

LILIAS TROTTER

Write Your Own Confession

1. How are you bursting for breakthrough?

2. What is it costing you?

3. Are there ways you need to confess resentment?

4. Are there ways God is asking you to stretch your imagination and confess your trust once more?

BUSY

The hand-scrawled list beside my keyboard says:

- roof
- Easter, baptisms
- bookkeeping, property
- tenants
- orientation packet for incoming elders
- new service

Some of these are the reasons I was drawn into ministry. They're hard work but work that restores me even as it tires me. Preparing for Easter, for baptisms, for developing leaders and shaping worship services is work of mess and mystery. It can't be forced, but I create open space in my mind and calendar to watch and listen. It's the humbling and glorious work of any creative endeavor, one you know you have a part in but is not yours to do alone, work that you have to devote your time and energy to but that will not be tamed. It falls into place when it will.

Then there are things that have made their way onto my list (and into my mind) that are the kind of work I am not equipped for. I'm accustomed to doing things I don't want to do. I'm not a delicate diva demanding that I only do what's on my job description. But these things drain the energy that I need to do the things that *are* on my job description. Chasing contractors to get roofing quotes, figuring out how to move around investments to pay for those quotes, finding new ways to divide the tasks of bookkeeping and property management, negotiating with tenants who rent our hall—to say I don't enjoy them is not enough. I am not good at them, and no amount of trying and being flexible and teachable is giving me the capacity they require of me.

And the energy it takes to try to find that capacity is draining the natural capacities I *do* have. It's draining my joy for all of it.

Of course, many of these tasks are not my job to complete. In a small church, things fall to the pastor that are not pastoral tasks. And it's the pastor's job to even discern whether to take them. And when the pastor discerns that they can't take on a task, it's then the pastor's job to find someone else to do the task. And in a small, aging church, there are so few to ask.

When I say yes to everything that comes my way, it's a sure sign I'm not getting enough rest. Yes, I have the responsibility to be sure I don't have too much to do. But even keeping that balance is a lot of work. Even discerning what is and isn't mine to do is a lot of work. Even finding others to take on tasks (and training them to do the tasks) is a lot of work.

> *Father, I don't even know what to pray.*
>   *I'm just tired of being busy.*
>   *I sigh in your direction.*
>   *Provide the help I need even to know the places I need*
> *help and the places to find it.*
>   *Amen.*

"Any survey of the biographies of the men and women of the Bible who were caught up in this drama reveals that God is not easy on those who are called. At the end of their lives, the best of them were beaten up and taped together. It almost seems that they had been overused in the biblical story. But all of them seemed content. That's because their joy came from being God's blessing along the way."[2]

M. CRAIG BARNES

Write Your Own Confession

1. How do you need to sigh in God's general direction at the moment?

2. Create your confession of sighs.

IN NEED OF ENCOURAGEMENT

"How was your Good Friday service?" my neighbor calls.

"Fine. Good, I think," I respond, then add: "It's kinda like parenting. You do what you can and hope for the best."

I'm keeping it light, but it's not a joke.

Her question makes me look back on the morning's service for the first time. It was Good Friday. Of course no one stopped to give feedback when the service was over. They were deep in contemplation. At least I hope they were. I hope they were so taken by a line from a hymn, a word from Scripture that they needed to rush home to pray. Of course if they've been struck in a new way by an old truth, their mind won't be on the voice that spoke it or the hands that typed it into the liturgy back on Thursday morning. I don't want them to feel the need to thank me. I want them to be thanking God. I want to bring a word, not be the Word.

At the same time, Paul said, "Let us consider how we may spur one another on toward love and good deeds, not giving up meeting together, as some are in the habit of doing, but encouraging one another—and all the more as you see the Day approaching" (Hebrews 10:24-25, NIV). Christians are supposed to proactively spur one another on. Not for the sake of puffing up egos but to help us keep faithful to love and good deeds. We're supposed to do it even more as we see the Day approaching. The longer the Day takes to arrive, the more we (I) need that kind of spurring on.

There are some services when several folks stop me to say, "Wow, what a wonderful service." I smile and say, "I'm so glad it was a blessing for you," careful not to make it about me. On those days I'm genuinely glad for an answer to my prayer that something in each service might connect with each heart gathered.

There are some services when someone says, "You're a great preacher!" I never know what to say to that. Evaluating preaching in that way feels to me like saying, "You're a really great talker" after having just heard that person wrap up in a wonderful, engaging conversation, reducing something immersive and relational to a skill set.

The best times are when someone says, "I'm moved/fascinated/surprised by that truth in the service today." Something that stirred in me while writing the sermon is now stirring in them. I hoped it was true, so I spoke it, and now, when I see it shining in their eyes, I believe it even more. Maybe they're also seeing how it shines in my eyes. Neither of us created it, and we know it.

This is why I hunger for feedback. There was a time when I needed it to feed my insecurities (although praise never seemed to make a dent in them). But now it's different. I'm only one small being seeing with one small set of eyes, hoping the perspective I bring is also real for everyone but not knowing for sure if it is.

Sometimes it doesn't happen right after the service. So I can't read too much into the silences. Silence can mean "I'm deep in contemplation" or "I need time to think" or "I'm bored" or "I'm perturbed." Silence is also what we get if our work is making no difference whatsoever. I haven't yet learned to discern the difference between the silences.

Beyond the way feedback gives me insight into how God is working in this place, is it okay that I also need encouragement, the kind that keeps me true to my calling, spurs me on to love and good deeds? This is hard, hard work. Some days I don't know if anything I do makes any difference. I don't want to make it about me, and at the same time, Jesus was an actual person, walking on particular feet, speaking with a unique voice. If the obedient actions, the courageous proclamation of one person aren't important, don't make any difference, why bother doing this at all? So much of what's happening here wouldn't be happening if one small person weren't attending to it every day.

So sometimes I pray for encouragement. When I've been close

to giving up, I know I need something to keep me true. God created the church because he knew we need one another to remain faithful to truth in a world that lies to us daily. So is it okay for me to need the church in that way? I wonder if this is a part of how I'm supposed to lead people in discipleship, if occasionally, after having first discerned my motives and being careful not to burden people, I let a little of my tiredness or discouragement leak out and let them pray for me. So they can also see the power of their own small words.

The funny thing is, there are moments when someone catches me off guard with a torrent of positivity. It's not praise for my skill or talent but deep encouragement that tells me my labor is not in vain, that God is taking my efforts and making them something. It's all too much for me. I can't take it in. Partly because it feels too good to be true, and partly because I'm living in a moment when church leaders are told not to let anything go to their heads. I want it to go to my heart.

God of all courage, of all encouragement,
When I'm in a feedback desert, let me turn to you to
learn how I'm doing, who I am.
When praise falls from nowhere, let me know how to
receive what is from you in it.
I don't need to hear that I'm perfect, that I have nothing
to learn.
I need to hear that whatever I am is something you
can use.
I want to hear that small things I did helped bring the
Kingdom.
I want to know that your Spirit is working through this
tired body, this small voice, no more than your Spirit works
through any body or voice. But also no less.
Amen.

"Say to my soul, 'I myself am your rescue.' Say it in such a way that I hear it."[3]

AUGUSTINE

Write Your Own Confession

1. How are you needing encouragement?

2. How is God inviting you to confess what is not healthy? How is God asking you to receive his encouragement?

3. Confess to God what you need from him.

NEEDING A WORD

I walk to this rock every morning. But today the draw to sit is powerful, like the rock has lassoed my insides and is tugging me downward. So I sit. And I sit. And I wait.

I need a word from the Lord. He feels far away. I need help that's not coming. I need guidance that's not confusing. Why did God want me to sit on this rock? Did he want my attention? My ears are open—I'm listening!

But then not a word but a weight. A kind pressure on my shoulders. *Just sit. Just be. Have you noticed yet the warmth of this sun, the way it draws the tension from the back of your neck? Have you noticed yet the way a rock can absorb restless energy? You're paying attention with your ears, but I don't want to bombard you with more words. My hope is not to give you more to think about. Pay attention with your skin. Pay attention with your lungs. Draw me in, and let me draw out everything that makes your heart race.*

Yes, you have much to do. But not now. For now, sit on a rock by the river. And be.

You will find rest for your soul.

God,

I confess that I have my own ideas of what I need from you.

And when it doesn't come in that form, I question your guidance and your comfort.

Let me always have a great imagination for who you are and what you could do

without writing the script for you.

Let me trust not "that God will do . . ." but that God is.
Amen.

"Jesus says that if we love him and fulfill his commandments, he will love us and disclose himself to us. This is not a question of a theology or a teaching but a question of life, of receiving Jesus as a real person, as the Son of Man who wants to love us and reveal himself to us. When we dwell in Jesus, he will dwell in us, and we can say like Paul the Apostle, 'I live, yet not I, but Christ liveth in me.'"[4]

J. HEINRICH ARNOLD

Write Your Own Confession

1. What do you need to cry out to the God who doesn't seem to be listening?

2. What do you need to confess to make yourself open to the possibility he is already answering?

PIONEERING

I had the dream again. The one I've had a million times.

I was responsible for a baby but somehow I'd forgotten. In the dream I'm just going about my life and suddenly I realize I was supposed to be caring for a baby. Where did this baby come from? Why haven't I been taking care of it? Did I forget? Or was it just left there without anyone telling me to watch it? Regardless, it's not been fed or bathed or cared for in any way for a distressing amount of time. It was supposed to be my job to have been doing all those things for all that time. And I haven't been.

I often imagine my perfect job: running arts programming part-time for a local library. The worst thing that can happen is that you run out of glue. In a job like that, you can't do much damage to people. I imagine a predictable job like that might mean I'd have time to always be pleasant, available, prepared for every eventuality.

But instead God seems to always put me in stuck places that need unsticking or places in crisis that need renewal or unsustainable places that need reimagining (in fact, it seems to be the place he puts every Christian leader at this point in the life of the church). I have a love/hate relationship with the metaphor of building the plane midflight. It's not a scary enough image when you also feel you're being asked to reimagine the sky.

I love a creative challenge, but I'd rather not be wrapped up in it. I'd rather watch the creativity taking place on paper. I'd rather not be rethinking the whole world I'm part of, including my own role in it. I love the feeling of stretching my mind to encompass new possibilities. I'd rather not be asked to stretch my very self. I like the idea of sitting on the potter's stool, but don't ask me to slide onto the spinning wheel.

I'm a settler at heart. I know how to enter a space and welcome folks and be a reassuring presence. I know how to shape a culture through slow, deep contemplation of who we are and who we're becoming and lead in that direction over the course of many years.

But God seems to see pioneer potential in this settler. He seems to see capacities in me I don't see. There's never enough time and space to feel prepared for my days. Because we're reimagining everything as we go, so every meeting, every sermon, every day brings moments I can't possibly prepare for. I could ensure this baby was well cared for if I just knew what it would need from day to day. I could promise to always be ready, never say the wrong thing if I just had the script ahead of time.

I'm growing in my capacity for chaos. I'm clinging like crazy to Jesus' promise "Don't be worried about what you'll say" (Matthew 10:19, author's paraphrase). I'm adding to it "or do or decide or become." And I'm learning there are some whose whole lives feel chaotic—not just their work but their health and homelife and past and future—and I want to be available to them.

This week I watched an episode of a brilliant TV series.[5] It began with an obstetrician waking in his car, disoriented, to finally figure out that instead of driving home the night before, he'd collapsed with exhaustion in the driver's seat in the hospital parking lot. And now he wakes to a new workday before him, requiring new things of him with no regard for his lack of breakfast. Before he can even get into the hospital, he encounters a woman giving birth on the driveway and his workday begins—one crisis after another, requiring him to regularly scrub other people's bodily fluids from his skin. In the middle of it all, he makes a split-second decision that endangers the life of a child, and his boss calls him to account. When he apologizes, as he should, I know it's the right thing to do. But at the same time, I want to scream, "But how can he possibly perform well when his work is so crazy, demands more than any human could do? The boss should be apologizing to him for asking so much of him!" To give all you have and discover it's not enough is beyond humbling.

Literally giving birth asks more of you than you ever expected: It scars you, and somehow along the way, as much as you adore those children, despite your best efforts, you also scar them. The scars are hidden in all the gifts you've given them. You can't give them those gifts, draw them that close, without risking messing them up a bit in the process. It would be simpler, safer to keep them at a distance and ensure your care for them was consistently mediocre instead of a flamboyant emptying of self at the risk of harm. How can you ensure someone else is not harmed when you're throwing your own, whole self in with little regard for your own safety? When you feel like you're falling, falling, how can you ensure the child you carry is not feeling the fall?

I remember now (with a curious smile): The baby in my dreams is somehow always okay. Although every dream brings me to that heart-stopping moment when I discover I've been unwittingly neglecting a baby, the baby always seems fine, oblivious to my incompetence. I cling to this crazy grace. I've always thought grace is the button I get to push at the end of my life that opens the door to heaven, even though I don't deserve it. But I'm opening to the possibility that grace is the fluid in which we swim, that fills up every empty space. That grace takes every mistake, every scar, every misstep and does something new and sacred with it. Often it's something that mystifies and mortifies me. But it doesn't kill me.

> *Gracious God,*
>   *You know whom you called to this place, to these people,*
> *to this constant change.*
>   *Give pioneer courage to this settler's heart.*
>   *Help me build the thing I can't yet see with words I don't*
> *yet have.*
>   *In every way I feel unsettled, may it teach me the*
> *experience of the unsettled.*

*Perhaps, when the world and the church are in upheaval,
we're all pioneers.*

Help us settle in your pioneering heart.

Amen.

"The Church lives between the time of Christ's death and resurrection and the final consummation of all things which he will bring; she is a pilgrim people, always on the way towards a promised goal; here she does not have a continuing city but seeks one to come. On the way Christ feeds her with Word and Sacraments, and she has the gift of the Spirit in order that she may not lose the way."[6]

UNITING CHURCH IN AUSTRALIA, *BASIS OF UNION*

Write Your Own Confession

1. What feels like too much change?
   How would you rather feel settled?

2. Does that discomfort come between you and God?

3. How might the discomfort be a place where you need God?
   Confess that however you can.

LEADING FROM FAITH

"They triumphed . . .
by the blood of the Lamb
and by the word of their testimony."
REVELATION 12:11, NIV

[Our] basic frameworks were formed by the socio-cultural paradigms coming primarily from the social sciences, psychology, and the business world. . . . We have all been formed, whether in church or seminary or other social structures—to be blind to God's agency. . . . [What we need is] leaders whose imagination and practices are shaped far less by the existent models of human agency and far more about discerning the ways in which God is present as agent in the process of calling into being the kingdom. . . . God is active [and] we are invited to participate, to join with God.

MARK LAU BRANSON AND ALAN ROXBURGH,
LEADERSHIP, GOD'S AGENCY, AND DISRUPTIONS

Outside my window there's a man spraying for termites. He's whistling. I'm envious. I suppose that whistling at work is possible when you know what you're doing. I've rarely felt that way in ministry. A termite guy is given training and tools and a uniform, and he's good to go. The tools I've been given rarely still apply to my work.[1]

There was a time when the role of the Christian leader was a pretty stable one, when the shape of a congregation or worship service felt preset. There was a time when the textbooks leaders read in seminary still were applicable by the time they retired. After all, we're part of an ancient tradition, interpreting a timeless text. So this calling to Christian leadership has attracted the settlers among us, the personalities who love history, who know how to plant themselves in a place and invest for a long time. If we'd wanted constant change and adventure, we might have instead become traveling evangelists or foreign missionaries. But now, whether we like it or not, we're all pioneers. And it doesn't look like things are going to stabilize any time soon.

For years we've prayed for change, but this is too much at once. It feels like God has thrown us into the deep end. But by God's grace, this desperation can become our opportunity to learn the very skill we need in this moment. The disruption holds the potential to teach us the very posture this secular world most needs to see from us—actual dependence on the power of a transcendent God.

But when we find ourselves thrown into the deep end, it's no small thing to give up our own efforts. It's only reasonable that we want to look like competent swimmers, able to save ourselves and others from the sinking. In crisis there's pressure on us to be competent. And our efforts to be competent have made us mediocre swimmers who have forgotten that human beings float. We've lost the ability to perceive the power all around us that can save us all. So how can we unlearn the world's ways of being professional to relearn the kinds of skills required for partnering with an unseen force? Can we stop playing savior long enough to learn the subtle art of engaging mess and mystery?

I want very much for this book to be practical and relatable, to leave readers with next steps, not vague ideals. I'm tempted to end the book with "Six Easy Ways to Lead from Faith." It would be satisfying for you and for me. But there are innumerable ways to lead from faith, and not one of them is easy.

My hope is that my confessions, as personal and unique to me as they are, are a different kind of practical, in a way that puts flesh on the kinds of wrestling we all must do.

The practical skill this confessing is teaching me is this: to learn to feel in my body the difference between self-reliance and God-reliance. I'm learning to catch myself turning from the risky reaching out, to feel those outstretched roots knotting inward to suck me dry again. I'm growing in my capacity for the discomfort of choosing again to stretch out for everything I need from a source I can't see or understand.

Every day this work gives us moments to navigate the messiness of relational realities where we have to ask God, *What are you doing in my life that's just for me, and what part do you want me to share? How can I share in a way that's healthy and not codependent or manipulative?* We'll have to figure out the complexity of power dynamics, how to share God's leading of us without coercing others. Every day gives us a chance to understand the complexities of ego, know how to invite others into our own experiences of God without centering ourselves, and find the Christlike kind of authority that only comes from emptying ourselves. Every day requires us to welcome the quirkiness of personality and emotion (our own and others'), watching Jesus reveal himself through our own ordinary, particular ways of being. And every single moment, we'll get to discover new ways to need God, letting those amateur skills of loving and waiting and praying and sharing testimonies enliven our professional work. All this takes tiny, daily choices of faith.

The fact remains: Faith begets faith. We've tried sharing Jesus through our own ideas, doctrines, rules, programs. Some of it has worked. Much of it has not enabled the transformed lives or vibrant communities that Scripture promises. When we can no longer cruise on "the way it's always been done," when the old language and ways of understanding Scripture begin to lose their meaning, our greatest skill will be to remember to ask once more where the Spirit is leading and say yes over and over. If you hear my passion, hear it as the passion of a new convert. I've chosen a new way but am still figuring out what on earth I've chosen. After years of learning how to be good at this work, I'm choosing the beginner mind, at great risk. But because I see a power at work beyond my own, I'm willing to keep taking that risk.

So instead of leaving you with "Six Easy Ways to Lead from Faith," I want to leave you with a story, one that changed my life and work forever.

My conversion to this way of leading came on a Monday morning. When I answered the phone, I had no idea that call might become one of the most powerful, transformative moments of my ministry experience. And the most remarkable thing about the power was that I know I did very little to make the powerful thing possible.

Lely's voice on the end of the line was quietly intense as she poured out her story of emotional, spiritual, and physical torment.[2] She'd tried everything that promised to save her life and everything that might end her life, and she was turning to me as a last effort. I felt the gravity of what she was asking of me, and my heart raced under the weight of it. I began (perhaps partly to share the burden) with "I feel that I should say I'm not a doctor or a psychologist. Are you seeing professionals in those fields?" She said she was.

I gulped. What on earth could I offer her? What is it that I, as a professional Christian, can offer? All week I'd been feeling ineffective in my ministry efforts. How could my feeble skills possibly save a life?

The words came.

"A pastor can offer you something different from a doctor or psychologist. But it won't mean much unless you believe God is powerful," I said.

(I wonder now if I was hoping she'd say she didn't believe so I'd be protected from the disappointment of more ineffectiveness.)

But before I could even finish, Lely surprised me by saying, "I do! I do believe God is powerful!"

What on earth was I supposed to say now? She'd told me the depth of her darkness and the power of her faith. I'm a professional people helper, someone who claims to work for One who does miracles. I wanted to fix her, to see healing for her sake . . . and for mine. My overwhelming inadequacy leaked out in a tiny, silent prayer: *What now, Lord?*

And then in the darkness of my spiraling desire to feel competent as a professional, there was a small point of light: *Just say what you believe about her.*

And so I opened my mouth and let these words pour out: "I believe you are precious in God's sight. I believe you are loved and worthy. I believe God made you for a reason, that he smiled when you were born. Your life is unlike any other life that has ever been or ever will be, and there is a unique way God wants to show himself to the world through your gifts and personality."

And then I remembered Psalm 139, so I read that too. That's all I did. That's all I knew to do. So that's all I did.

And then I heard it—a change in her voice: "I feel something lifting." In the months since that day, Lely has told me how on that first phone call a kind of electricity was coursing through her body, bringing her back to life. She tells the story over and over, describing a spell being broken, one that had drawn her to her grave for sixteen years. That electric current has been strong enough to get her through months of battling a broken mental-health system, relational dysfunction, through therapy and prayer and Bible study. It remains in her still, lighting up her eyes as she speaks about God's work in her. I watch Lely tell her story in psychiatric facilities and on buses in a way that's somehow at the same time disarming and disruptive. She can't keep it to herself. Those who have known her awhile want to know how that shrunken lady became so radiant.

Both of us know that whatever happened that day was not

entirely our doing. Whatever power we experienced was not our power. Her confession of belief in God's power gave me courage to do my work. And my confession of belief in God's love for her spoke new possibilities into her life. Neither of us can take the credit. But both of us can celebrate how the other's faith in a powerful God made a space for him to do miracles.

This way of following is simple—not easy, but simple. It means paying attention to how God leads through Scripture, through prayer, through the community and simply saying yes, whether we understand where it will lead . . . or not. It's risky and costly, of course, but we've been promised that's our way (Matthew 16:24).

If it's normal to follow in this way in our personal faith, why would we expect it to be any different in our work of teaching others to follow? There are moments when I panic: *Can this really be the right way to do important things? So much in my education and culture would ridicule this as the way to anything serious!* When these fears arise, I remind myself: *Everything about this work is based on the premise that there is a powerful God at work in and through the gathered communities that bear his Spirit. Every story of the church's founding came from surprising encounters and ordinary human responses. They became transcendent, transformative moments that began with simply paying attention, saying yes, and telling the stories of God's work.*

But don't hear me saying I always fully believe. Belief is not feeling or understanding. Belief is choosing. Somehow *He has great faith* has become a statement about someone's own strength. But to have great faith is not to have great capacity except the capacity to choose to say yes to God. It may not be an easy choice. And we may not like or understand it. But to choose it is within our capacity. Faith is not our strength, it's our awareness of where our strength ends, a kind of stubborn refusal to pretend we're strong and a muscle memory of what to do when we're not. This kind of faith is not beyond the average person. Regardless of how much certainty or closeness to God we feel, if faith is an act of will, it's always in our control. We can choose to say, "I don't know what God has in store (and sometimes I wonder if he's listening), but Scripture says God is powerful, his Spirit is active in us and the world, and that when his people get together and share the Good News, miracles can happen. So let's live as if that is true."

If following and leading by faith begins with saying yes over and over, we have great hope in this moment of crisis. As we question everything we've known and believed, as we watch the crumbling of all our personal, congregational, and institutional practices and traditions, when so much about contemporary Christian leadership feels impossible, this way of leading is hopeful.

It's hopeful because it's not just for the most charismatic or educated or driven. When faith becomes the greatest impetus of our leadership, we suddenly have a more numerous and diverse array of leaders available in every congregation. And this way of leadership is naturally humble and collaborative, growing from a deep awareness of our need for God and for one another. It makes us less ashamed that we don't bring all that's needed here and more ready to welcome the gifts of all. It creates a capacity for risk and grace. And underneath it all, this way of leading has a deep integrity, one not based on the unspoken assumption that it's all up to us. When we approach the work of leading through the lens of following God, the hard parts of the work train us in that skill all the more.

What if the thing our folks most need from us is to see our own need for God? And what if the thing the world most needs from us is to watch our faces alight with something that makes no worldly sense? Will we deny them that? Or will we risk letting our faith be seen, feeble and unimpressive though it may be? In moments of confusion and clarity, of surprise and joy, in moments of waiting, of wrestling, of desperation and darkness, will we share how we're choosing to hope and follow? When we do, we may be saved from the weight of trying to be God. We may be saved to follow, and we may find ourselves surrounded by others wanting whatever they see in us, in all its joyous messiness. In this moment in the story of the church, when it's easy to believe these are her final days, perhaps our longing to see her healed and flourishing may be the very place she begins to heal and flourish.

It takes faith to keep reading (and teaching) a Bible that says hard and confusing things.

It takes faith to stop to pray in the middle of a tense business meeting when you just want to look like the competent leader who can fix the problem.

It takes faith to send out enthusiastic invitations for events that may or may not be a success.

It takes faith to lead the singing because someone has to do it, even though singing in public is your greatest fear.

It takes faith to press against opposition when you want to be liked.

It takes faith to preach your conviction when you know you'll lose the offerings that pay your salary.

It takes faith to draw a line for the sake of the community when you know it will step on someone's toes.

It takes faith to model waiting on God's direction when people want answers from you now.

It takes faith to confess you're not feeling close to God when people want to rely on your strength.

It takes faith to cast a vision of something you haven't yet seen (so that the vision might become a reality for all to see, including you).

It takes faith to say "God is good" when you feel like giving up.

It takes faith to rest when you want to look (and feel) productive and efficient.

It takes faith to stay when your survival instincts say, *Get away from here!*

(and to go when you just want to stay).

It takes faith not to take things personally when they feel so personal.

It takes faith to proclaim healing when all you see is brokenness.

It takes faith to proclaim provision when all you see is scarcity.

It takes faith to pay attention to still, small (often confusing) voices more than the clamoring calls for clarity (some of which are happening in your own head).

Living this kind of life that every day goes against our comfort and self-preservation in all these (and many other) ways would generally crush a person.[3] But if we choose it every day out of obedience, out of joining Jesus in his emptying, we also come to know his filling. So in that sacred place after what feels like death, God meets us, as he met Jesus in the tomb, and says, "That place that seemed beyond hope is the place I do my best work."

ACKNOWLEDGMENTS

Thank you, Jamie, for saying yes with me, over and over. And for the tea.

Thank you to Winn and Tryg and the Holy Presence Cohort "frauds" for joining me in lakeside dancing and impromptu pennywhistle parades and all manner of cheese chasing.

Thank you to Mum and Dad and Wendy and Meryem and Deb and Cheryl and Charlene and Sandie and Meg and Jan and Karen and Dom and Emily for hearing my confessions. And not flinching.

For all the good folks at Eastside Christian Church, Bridgetown Church of Christ, University Christian Church, and St Lucia Uniting Church.

To every fellow laborer who ever worked alongside me. I'm learning how much of the work of the church happens among leaders, behind the scenes, in the ways we give one another grace. Thank you for the grace you've given me.

NOTES

INTRODUCTION

1. Andrew Root, *The Pastor in a Secular Age: Ministry to People Who No Longer Need a God*, Ministry in a Secular Age, vol. 2 (Grand Rapids: Baker Academic, 2019), xvi, xix.

2. See George Ritzer, *The McDonaldization of Society: Into the Digital Age*, 10th ed. (Thousand Oaks, CA: Sage, 2021); John Drane, *The McDonaldization of the Church: Consumer Culture and the Church's Future* (Macon, GA: Smyth and Helwys, 2001); and C. Christopher Smith and John Pattison, *Slow Church: Cultivating Community in the Patient Way of Jesus* (Downers Grove, IL: InterVarsity Press, 2014).

3. Eugene H. Peterson, *The Contemplative Pastor: Returning to the Art of Spiritual Direction* (Grand Rapids: Eerdmans, 1993), 64.

4. "The earliest sense of *amateur* ('one that has a marked fondness, liking, or taste') is strongly connected to its roots: the word came into English from the French *amateur*, which in turn comes from the Latin word for 'lover' (*amator*)." *Merriam-Webster*, s.v. "amateur (*n.*)," accessed November 8, 2023, https://www.merriam-webster.com/dictionary/amateur.

CHAPTER ONE | CONFESSING UNBELIEF, CONFESSING BELIEF

1. Helpful language borrowed from James K. A. Smith: https://divinity.uchicago.edu/sightings/articles/james-ka-smiths-cultural-liturgies.

2. Brenda B. Colijn, *Images of Salvation in the New Testament* (Downers Grove, IL: IVP Academic, 2010), 94.

CHAPTER TWO | I WANT TO BE IN CONTROL

1. Teresa of Ávila, *Interior Castle*, trans. and ed. E. Allison Peers (New York: Image Books, 2004), 29.

2. James Finley, *Thomas Merton's Path to the Palace of Nowhere: The Essential Guide to the Contemplative Teachings of Thomas Merton* (Boulder, CO: Sounds True, 2002), audiobook.

3. Oswald Chambers, "Yes—But . . . !," in *My Utmost for His Highest*, updated ed. (Grand Rapids: Our Daily Bread Publishing, 1992), May 30, https://utmost.org/updated/yes-but.

4. Stanley Hauerwas, "Being with the Wounded: Pastoral Care within the Life of the Church," stanleyhauerwas.org, January 11, 2019, https://stanley hauerwas.org/being-with-the-wounded-pastoral-care-within-the-life -of-the-church.

5. David E. Fitch, *Faithful Presence: Seven Disciplines That Shape the Church for Mission* (Downers Grove, IL: IVP Books, 2016), 30.

CHAPTER THREE | I WANT TO FORCE MIRACLES

1. Name has been changed to protect privacy.

2. Anna Carter Florence, *Preaching as Testimony* (Louisville: Westminster John Knox Press, 2007), 158.

3. Dietrich Bonhoeffer, *Life Together: The Classic Exploration of Christian Community* (New York: HarperOne, 2009), 17.

4. Nick Cave and Seán O'Hagan, *Faith, Hope and Carnage* (New York: Picador, 2023), 271. Quote by Cave in a conversation between O'Hagan and Cave.

5. Evelyn Underhill, *The Spiritual Life: Great Spiritual Truths for Everyday Life* (Oxford: Oneworld, 1999), 64.

6. Marilynne Robinson, *Gilead* (New York: Picador, 2020), 27–28.

7. Augustine, *Confessions*, trans. Sarah Ruden (New York: Modern Library, 2018), 3.

CHAPTER FOUR | I WANT TO KNOW OUTCOMES

1. Annie Dillard, *Pilgrim at Tinker Creek* (New York: HarperCollins, 2013), 245.

2. Dietrich Bonhoeffer, *The Cost of Discipleship*, trans. R. H. Fuller (New York: Macmillan, 1951), 51.

3. Bono, *Surrender: 40 Songs, One Story* (New York: Alfred A. Knopf, 2022), 137.

CHAPTER FIVE | I WANT TO FEEL SUCCESSFUL

1. Thomas Merton, *New Seeds of Contemplation* (New York: New Directions, 2007), 297.

2. Augustine, *Confessions*, trans. Sarah Ruden (New York: Modern Library, 2018), 90.

3. Hildegard of Bingen, *Scivias*, trans. Columba Hart and Jane Bishop (New York: Paulist Press, 1990), 310.

4. Mother Teresa, as quoted in James Finley, *Thomas Merton's Path to the Palace of Nowhere: The Essential Guide to the Contemplative Teachings of Thomas Merton* (Boulder, CO: Sounds True, 2002), audiobook.

5. Edwin H. Friedman, *A Failure of Nerve: Leadership in the Age of the Quick Fix* (New York: Seabury Books, 2007), 233.

CHAPTER SIX | I WANT TO BE FREE

1. John Koenig, *The Dictionary of Obscure Sorrows* (New York: Simon and Schuster, 2021), 47.
2. Thomas Merton, *New Seeds of Contemplation* (New York: New Directions, 2007), 34.
3. Peter L. Steinke, *How Your Church Family Works: Understanding Congregations as Emotional Systems* (Lanham, MD: Rowman and Littlefield, 2006), 128.
4. David Hansen, *The Art of Pastoring: Ministry without All the Answers*, rev. ed. (Downers Grove, IL: IVP Books, 2012), 36.
5. Thomas à Kempis, *The Imitation of Christ*, rev. ed. trans. and ed. Joseph N. Tylenda (New York: Vintage Books, 1998), 104.
6. Henri J. M. Nouwen, "Living with Hope," in *Bread for the Journey: A Daybook of Wisdom and Faith* (New York: HarperOne, 2006), January 16.
7. Evelyn Underhill, "God's Agents in the Real World," in *Advent with Evelyn Underhill*, ed. Christopher L. Webber (Harrisburg, PA: Morehouse Publishing, 2006), December 7.
8. Philippians 2:17, NIV.
9. Romans 12:1, NRSV.

CHAPTER SEVEN | I WANT TO FEEL STRONG

1. Frederick Buechner, *Telling the Truth: The Gospel as Tragedy, Comedy, and Fairy Tale* (New York: HarperSanFrancisco, 1977), 68.
2. Mark Lau Branson and Alan J. Roxburgh, *Leadership, God's Agency, and Disruptions: Confronting Modernity's Wager* (Eugene: Cascade Books, 2021), 22.
3. Walter Brueggemann, *The Prophetic Imagination*, 2nd ed. (Minneapolis: Fortress Press, 2001), 118.
4. Helpful language from Susan Scott, *Fierce Conversations: Achieving Success at Work and in Life, One Conversation at a Time*, rev. ed. (New York: New American Library, 2017), chap. 6.
5. Soraya Chemaly, *Rage Becomes Her: The Power of Women's Anger* (New York: Atria, 2019), 295.
6. James Finley, *Thomas Merton's Path to the Palace of Nowhere: The Essential Guide to the Contemplative Teachings of Thomas Merton* (Boulder, CO: Sounds True, 2002), audiobook.
7. Marva J. Dawn, *Powers, Weakness, and the Tabernacling of God* (Grand Rapids: Eerdmans, 2001), 163.
8. Quoted in Ellen Vaughn, *Becoming Elisabeth Elliot* (Nashville: B&H, 2020), 268. (As Vaughn notes, this poem was "transliterated in part from the Middle English.")

CHAPTER EIGHT | I WANT TO GIVE UP

1. Lilias Trotter quoted at Miriam Rockness (blog), "Tell 'Em about the Dream!" May 30, 2018, https://ililiastrotter.wordpress.com/2018/05/30/tell-em-about-the-dream.

2. M. Craig Barnes, *The Pastor as Minor Poet: Texts and Subtexts in the Ministerial Life* (Grand Rapids: Eerdmans, 2009), 103.

3. Augustine, *Confessions*, trans. Sarah Ruden (New York: Modern Library, 2018), 7.

4. J. Heinrich Arnold, *Discipleship: Living for Christ in the Daily Grind*, expanded ed. (Rifton, NY: Plough, 2011), 248.

5. *This Is Going to Hurt.*

6. The Uniting Church in Australia, *Basis of Union, Constitution and Regulations: 2018* (Sydney: Uniting Church in Australia Assembly, 2018), 10.

CHAPTER NINE | LEADING FROM FAITH

1. Sections of this chapter are adapted from an article previously published with Missio Alliance: Mandy Smith, "We're All Pioneers Now: Skills for the Unchartered Landscape of the 21st-Century Church," November 17, 2022, https://www.missioalliance.org/were-all-pioneers-now-skills-for-the-unchartered-landscape-of-the-21st-century-church. Included with permission.

2. Lely didn't only give me permission to use her name, she asked me to tell her story. This story is no amalgam. This is just the way it happened.

3. There are times when we just have to push through these discomforts as part of our call to take up our cross and follow. But there are also times when the pain of all these hard things is a sign it's time for a break or a sign that something needs to change (sometimes Jesus wept at the state of Jerusalem; other times he turned over tables—only he knows the difference, so be sure to ask him). It's hard to discern the difference, but please do so. Please don't read this list as one more message that making changes is never an option or that stopping is unfaithfulness. Your discomfort with how things are may be the impetus to disrupt the status quo for the sake of everyone involved.

NavPress is the book-publishing arm of The Navigators.

Since 1933, The Navigators has helped people around the world bring hope and purpose to others in college campuses, local churches, workplaces, neighborhoods, and hard-to-reach places all over the world, face-to-face and person-by-person in an approach we call Life-to-Life® discipleship. We have committed together to know Christ, make Him known, and help others do the same.®

Would you like to join this adventure of discipleship and disciplemaking?

- Take a Digital Discipleship Journey at **navigators.org/disciplemaking**.
- Get more discipleship and disciplemaking content at **thedisciplemaker.org**.
- Find your next book, Bible, or discipleship resource at **navpress.com**.

 @NavPressPublishing

 @NavPress

 @navpressbooks

CONFESSIONS

CONFESSIONS OF AN AMATEUR SAINT